THE WOULD-BE

Woodsman

PART I: From Show Me Launch to Woo Pig Sooie

WILLIAM W. WEST

WESTBOW
PRESS®
A DIVISION OF THOMAS NELSON
& ZONDERVAN

WestBow Press books may be ordered through booksellers or by contacting:

WestBow Press
A Division of Thomas Nelson & Zondervan
1663 Liberty Drive
Bloomington, IN 47403
www.westbowpress.com
1 (866) 928-1240

ISBN: 978-1-5127-6632-5 (sc)
ISBN: 978-1-5127-6631-8 (hc)
ISBN: 978-1-5127-6633-2 (e)

Library of Congress Control Number: 2016919787

Print information available on the last page.

WestBow Press rev. date: 12/28/2016

Contents

Some of the names and identifying details have been changed to protect the privacy of individuals.

The cover art drawing is by Billy West (WWW Jr.) when he was 12 years old and is used with his permission.

The photo of the downtown Springfield skyline in Chapter 1 dates from the 1930's and was printed in the un-copyrighted booklet produced by the Springfield Sesquicentennial Committee. This non-copyrighted work, "A Million Hours of Memories" was edited by Dick Grosenbaugh.

Before Thoughts

My life as the Would-be Woodsman has been rich and varied. This first volume takes us from the time I learned to read up through 1991 when we moved from Southwest Missouri to Central Arkansas. The fire of my desire to be a woodsman ignited with books and magazine articles about life in the outdoors. The fire of my desire to be a servant of the Most High God was ignited at the Cleveland Avenue Mission in the early 1960's.

These accounts are etched in my memory and heart so I guess that would make them my memoirs. Memoirs are usually the extraordinary accounts of the lives of important and significant people. I am neither. I am just a boy who wanted to be a woodsman, didn't know how to become one, and yet somehow did. The Would-be Woodsman could be described as a highly educated urban hillbilly.

In learning to be a successful woodsman I have learned some even more valuable lessons about being successful in life. I have learned a woodsman's success in the woods should never be his first priority.

The "Would-be" term I have chosen to describe myself speaks of desire. I would be a man after God's own heart; I would be a man being re-made (over my short lifetime) to be more like Jesus, my Savior; I would be a servant of the Most High God; I would be a husband who loves his wife and keeps his promises to God and her; I would be a father who by his love for them gives his children reasons to honor him; I would be a Granddaddy who lifts his grandchildren to God in prayer and leaves them a legacy of love and an example they can trust; and finally, I would be a woodsman.

I would like to thank my wife and children for allowing me time in the woods, time to get an education, and time to write. I am also grateful for how they have loved me through it all. They, along with my grandchildren, have taught me much about love.

As I look back on my life I realize how indebted I am to the many people who influenced my life for Christ and have taught me to serve Him. There are some I need to mention: Dr. Jim Joslin, Rev. John Doolittle, Rev. Max Edmonson, Chaplain Wally Hucabee, Chaplain Milton Tyler, Rev. Troy Rhoden, Rev. Tommy Harper, Rev. Leon Riddle, Dr. Phillip McClendon, and Dr. Ed Simpson. God used these men to teach me many things about Him and about myself. I am grateful for their impact on my life.

I would also like to thank some special friends, two who have already been promoted. Long ago my father, Truman West, in a candid and powerful moment said to me, "Son, if you can ever find a true friend hang onto them. I've never had one." I thank God for my father's sad advice for I have had seven such friends: Paul Roberts, Gene Bolt, Don Grove, Darrell Smith, John Lewis, Jacob Standley and Randy "Buzz" Bussard. What a blessing they have been to me.

Speaking of some other dear people in my life, I would like to ask the reader to be gracious in their judgments of those who introduced me to deer hunting. What may appear to be a lack of respect for game laws and ethical appreciation of the resources in their care is basically a product of their culture—not bad intentions.

I want to say I love and appreciate their willingness to share their lives and lands with me. I am indebted and grateful. Those early experiences of the Would-be Woodsman—even my ethical and spiritual failures—are dear to me. I always think of those family and friends with care and kindness. To protect them from being misunderstood I have chosen to refer to them by different names. I have never met anyone who is perfect, especially the guy in the mirror. Jesus is the only exception.

To any family and friends who might choose to read my memories, keep in mind that is what they are—memories. Memories are impressions left on our brains and interpreted by our hearts. If mine are different from yours on these accounts, please know I have shared them as honestly as memories can be shared. Remember, I am sixty years old.

I want to thank anyone who has picked up this book to give it a look. My hope is you will enjoy some of the funny stories and are encouraged or challenged by my struggle to live for the Lord through the mundane stuff of everyday life. I hope you will be able to sense how the woods, streams, lakes, and fields can be a powerful place to meet the Lord God. If the outdoor life is not for you, that is all right. This book may help you discover why someone you love gets so strangely excited about time in the woods. I hope so.

Finally, I want to thank God for all He has done, is doing, and will yet do to make the Would-be Woodsman's life so rich and real. The adventure never ends.

Chapter 1

In the Beginning

Downtown Springfield Skyline

I was born the second of six children to Truman and Mary West in the hot August of 1955. I don't remember it but my mother did and often told me about the mid-fifties drought years in Springfield, Missouri. We lived in downtown Springfield all of my childhood except for my second and third years. We spent those in the northern panhandle of Idaho where my dad was working in the zinc smelter mills. Brother Joe joined big sister Theresa and me there. My earliest memory is of being held by my father as the whole neighborhood stood in our Kellogg, Idaho, street while watching for Sputnik, whatever that was.

We returned to Springfield before I turned four and bought a two-bedroom house from my great aunt Geneva. Three more children—Jack, Richard, and Ramona—were added to the West family at 937 West Chestnut Street. The house was less than a mile from the city square. The downtown city skyline was a big part of my life as I grew up—always there like a beacon showing the way home.

I became enamored with the idea of hunting as a very young boy, even though I was city raised. The public library was always a big part of my summer life when it was not possible to play ball or swim. I was a sponge for fiction and biographies, especially if it had to do with the rugged outdoors.

Early in the month of August every year the Ozark Empire Fair would happen. Money from summer odd jobs would be hoarded for and spent on the fair. The rides were fun and the girls were pretty but my favorite attraction at the fair was always the Missouri Conservation Commission pavilion and displays. I pestered conservation officers with multiple questions and I would fill a bag with brochures and pamphlets on hunting, fishing, reptiles, bird watching, conservation, and anything else available.

I studied the fish in the tanks and imagined what it would be like to hook and land a giant bass or catfish. The display of snakes was both exciting and terrifying and there was always a penned menagerie of orphaned animals—foxes, raccoons, and deer who had survived their mothers' deaths. The whitetail fawns fascinated me.

These documents and experiences would spark dreams of outdoor adventure which were slow to develop flame for several good reasons. First, we lived in the very heart of Springfield in a small frame house on a 50 foot by 150 foot lot. Not much outdoor adventure there unless you count nearby Hobo Holler, which had its own peculiar hazards. Second, my Dad did not hunt. Third, I was afraid of the woods and things in the woods, particularly snakes.

When my uncle Lee came back from Vietnam he bought some beagles and began to learn rabbit hunting. He took me with him a few times and I loved it. This was long before the days of required hunter education and I am sure my lack of muzzle control had a great impact on the number of times (few) I was invited.

In high school my desire for the outdoors and hunting increased as I heard classmates describe their deer hunting adventures. *The Yearling,* by Marjorie Kinnan Rawlings, was required reading in my ninth grade English class. It sure beat *Romeo and Juliet.* The big English project for the spring semester was a research paper on a topic of choice. I did my paper on deer: elk, mule deer, whitetail deer, blacktail deer, and sub-species. It was a great learning experience and I think I received a B-. And yet, the only deer I had ever seen, dead or alive, were babies in a pen.

I knew if I were to ever become a woodsman, I would have to overcome my fear of the woods. The silence and loneliness of the rural outdoors overwhelmed me. I think many people who grow up in the city, with all of its noise and activity, are intimidated by the apparent quietness of the woods and fields. True, the outdoors are full of sounds but it takes a while for a city dweller to learn to hear them.

My family would do a river weekend several times during the summer. This usually amounted to paying a farmer a small fee to camp along their river frontage. Our favorites were the James, Finley, Sac, and Little Pomme de Terre rivers. The gathering usually involved 25 to 30 family members and friends. It was very simple camping and clean fun.

These family outings allowed me opportunities to deal with my love/hate relationship with the woods. I bought a makeshift rucksack and a canteen at the Army Surplus and would force myself to take solo exploratory hikes in the wooded hills along these rivers. It took some talking, but my mother finally consented for me to establish my own mini-campsite a couple of hundred yards from the bustle of the main camp when such a place was available. These activities also brought me up against my other fear, snakes.

I'm not sure where my snake phobia came from but I have some ideas. My dad had a healthy fear of snakes which he attributed to a nightmarish childhood experience. Growing up during the depression, he was the youngest of seven boys living in Springfield. A small lake at the city zoo was being drained and his brothers waded and caught fish by hand as the lake emptied. My father remembers he stood on the dam bank while one of his brothers, Julius or Preston, reached down into the outflow pipe. The brother screamed something about snakes and threw a handful of the creatures at his youngest sibling. Dad remembers, with horror, how the snakes landed on his head and shoulders. That story, however fractured it might be in my memory, was not wasted on me.

Another source of my phobia was one of those adventure books I had read. The title of the book has long since left me, but I remember it was the story about a city boy whose family inherited a rattlesnake-infested piece of country property.

The first major confrontation with my fear of snakes happened on one of my solo hikes out from a river weekend campsite. We were on a small stream near Tin Town, Missouri. Just after lunch I left out alone and climbed a steep wooded hill on the north side of the river. The view of the farmlands from that elevation was impressive to me and I sat for a while to enjoy the scene.

A lovely scene it surely was until I focused in closer to my perch and saw a large dark snake as it sunned on a rock outcropping about eight feet below me. Full blown panic seized me immediately and I bailed off of that little mountainside pretty much out of control. About halfway down my mind returned to me and I realized I was being foolish. Like Ralphy on the department store slide in *A Christmas Story* I slammed on the brakes and tried to grab saplings on my way down. On my third grab I came to a hand scraping halt and began to re-ascend the hill.

When I reached my previous location I discovered the snake was still there. After a long conversation with myself I identified the snake. It seemed to be a black snake. It was large, over five feet but not poisonous, and it appeared to pay me no attention. I watched for a while longer then chunked some rocks toward it just to show it who was boss. The snake finally moved off and so did I, in a different direction. Proud I was of my newfound courage as I leisurely returned to camp feeling "all was right with the world."

For the Christmas of my fifteenth year I received one of the few gifts from my childhood which remain with me to this day. It is a Japanese made single shot .410 shotgun. It actually belongs to my son now but is kept in my gun safe. Some of my neighborhood friends (outlaws-in-training) received semi-automatic .22's and as soon as one of us could drive we began going out to hunt rabbits and squirrels.

On one such outing two of the boys opened up on a doe deer that ran between them. I did not see the deer, which was never recovered, but I heard the war. It was not deer season and does were heavily protected in those days. Deer were just making a come-back in Missouri then. Even in my youthful ignorance I knew a .22 was both an illegal and unethical caliber for deer. The whole affair upset me and I soon found other things to do when a hunting trip was suggested by those guys.

In the summer before and during my senior year in high school I had the perfect job. I worked on the maintenance (weed and trash) crew in the utility owned park around Lake Springfield. At the end of the summer I was the only crew member retained to work after school and weekends to patrol, register boats, cleanup public outhouses, and lock up the recreation areas at night. I worked seven days-a-week and sunup to sundown on the weekends.

This is where I saw my first deer in the wild. I learned to watch for them, their tracks, and their spoor. This made me a deer hunter long before I ever carried a large caliber gun or bow into the woods. I read everything I could about whitetail deer and hunting. My park ranger-like job helped me to learn to feel comfortable in the outdoors. It was a great experience and I earned a buck sixty an hour to boot, which was good money for a seventeen year old boy in 1972.

Seven days after graduating from Central High School I began my long college career at the School of the Ozarks near Branson, Missouri. Most of the students there were from rural backgrounds and it seemed everyone had hunted deer, even the girls. I need to back up here for just a minute.

The summer I turned sixteen found me working odd jobs for the Greene County Baptist Association at their Grand Oak Mission Center. During that time the Association held a crusade at the Ozark Empire Fairgrounds arena with evangelist James Robison. I attended every service and after the Thursday evening meeting I made the biggest decision and best choice of my life. I repented of my sins and asked Jesus to become the Lord of my life and help me become the man He wanted me to be.

The same week I had noticed a very cute little gal who had come to the Mission Center with her youth group from Second Baptist Church. She helped teach Vacation Bible School. I remember clearly her dark hair, dark eyes, cool wire framed glasses, sailor hat, and pretty smile. A few weeks later the Baptist Association hired me to be the dishwasher and general flunky during their two weeks of camp at Baptist Hill near

Mount Vernon, Missouri. This young lady, whose name I discovered was Kathy Sanders, happened to be in the cabin of teenaged girls with my then current girlfriend, who was in the process of dumping me for the third time. I also discovered she had attended Central High with me the year before. How could I have overlooked such a pretty girl?

Not long after camp came my sixteenth birthday. I quickly acquired the required driver's license and insurance for operating the 35 dollar, 1960 white Volvo my dad had cobbled together from two salvaged cars. This new found freedom provided my red headed girlfriend ample opportunity to finish the dumping process. When school started I looked for Kathy Sanders. I couldn't help but notice her now. It turned out not only was she cute, but she was very smart and willing to help me with my Spanish lessons and other homework when I broke my right hand playing football in Physical Education class. So began a relationship that has gone the distance. Let me get back to 1973.

Chapter 2

1973: Successful Failure

I must have said something to Kathy about how I wanted to learn to deer hunt someday because her mother, Ardelle, mentioned the prospect to her father, Max. I was puzzled and a little hurt by his lack of enthusiasm about the possibility of my joining him, his sons, and extended family for their annual deer hunt near his childhood home in Ozark County. Years later, when I had my own teenaged daughters to guard and protect from guys like me, I came to perfectly understand that lack of enthusiasm. But Ardelle persisted and eventually Max caved in and I was invited to go.

I managed to coax my '62 Chevy back to Springfield after finishing classes and work at School of the Ozarks (S of O) on the Friday before deer season opened. I made it just in time to join Max, Jeff, and Greg (Kathy's brothers) for the trip down home. I didn't have a gun or deer tag but Max said not to worry about it. It seems many people in those parts didn't bother to buy a tag until they killed a deer, if they bothered at all. I was uneasy with that but hey, I was finally deer hunting and I certainly did not want to argue with the man I hoped would be my future father-in-law.

We made the two hour trip in the dark and arrived at his mother's house at Sycamore, just up the hill from the famed Hodgson Mill on Bryant Creek. I don't remember the sleeping arrangements but I do remember as I drifted off to sleep, I counted deer instead of sheep.

Day had just dawned when I woke up to the wonderful smells of

Kathy's grandmother preparing breakfast. I stepped out onto her front porch to take a look around. It was very foggy. I peered across the road in front of the house and noticed three deer drinking from a pond about 75 yards out. With great excitement I told everyone there were deer across the road.

The guns were still in the car and by the time they could be uncased and loaded, the deer were gone. Max instructed me how to use one of his 30-30's and placed me in a spot less than 200 yards from his mother's back door. He explained deer would sometimes move through this field and adjoining strip of woods as they prepared to cross the highway.

It was a long, nervous, and frustrating day. I took a break at lunchtime and a walk in the woods with Max's .22 in search of squirrels. I don't know for certain, but I think being in the field with a firearm not allowed for deer was illegal. It certainly is now in most places. It was difficult to sit on the wet ground most of the day but I tried nonetheless. I was very nervous about being an illegal hunter.

My imagination has always been a big one and I imagined every vehicle on the highway and every log floating down the rain-swollen Bryant Creek was a game warden ready to nab me. There certainly is truth to the Proverb that says, "The wicked flee when no one pursues . . . ." (Proverbs 28:1)

If anyone in Max's family doubted my immaturity as a woodsman, I clarified it for them by the end of the day. The only activity I noticed all day after the early morning deer citing was a very large cotton tailed rabbit as it bounced around the edge of the field between my post and Grandma Sanders' garden plot. It had rained quite a bit during the afternoon and I was wet, cold, and frustrated. When it was finally time to call it a day I started back to the house and once again the rabbit bounced out into the edge of the field. Immediately, I drew a bead on the rabbit at about 40 yards and fired.

What a kid thing to do. It was probably the first time I had ever fired a rifle (other than my Daisy). When I reached the rabbit and discovered my aim had been true I was momentarily proud of myself. I was surprised and impressed with how the .30 caliber bullet had nearly separated the rabbit's head from its body. Not thinking about the proximity to the house, I was also surprised when Kathy's uncle, who unbeknown to me, had been watching the road from his truck parked in front of his mother-in-law's house, came hustling through the brush and shouted "Did you get one?" My witty—I thought—answer was, "Yeah, a big buck."

About that time he got close enough to see me holding my prize. His response was something like, "What in the world! You said you killed a buck!" I meekly defended myself, "It is a buck—rabbit." What I thought was a good joke simply served to display my immaturity as a woodsman. I dressed the unfortunate bunny and presented it to Grandma Sanders who fried it along with bacon and sausage for breakfast the next morning.

On Sunday Max sent me across the road to sit just to the east of the pond where we had seen deer the previous morning. It was really foggy and visibility was less than forty feet. The sun finally rose and the fog began to slowly lift its cover from the brushy field I guarded. I heard a noise I imagined was the hoof beats of running deer. I pivoted toward the sound and brought the hammer of the rifle to full cock.

Dumb move. No deer materialized and no further deer-like sound was detected so I sat back down on the ground and leaned against a small oak tree. The fog continued to lift. My mind wandered back to wherever it had been.

My day dream was interrupted by a screen door slam and a man's shout. I jumped up and turned to the west and was startled to see a doe moving south across the field, broadside at less than 50 yards. Max had been watching out Grandma's front window and seen this doe as she walked right up the middle of Highway 181. He had moved onto the porch and frightened the doe, who then jumped the fence into the field with me. It was a good move for her.

Does were legal the first two days of the season that year, even if I wasn't. As I brought the gun to bear on the doe it discharged about halfway up and dealt death and destruction to an innocent bush about ten yards away. I was inexcusably unfamiliar with the rifle and I had left it on full cock. I was so stunned and embarrassed a second attempt was out of the question. Max was kind enough about the whole deal but obviously unimpressed. I felt bad.

I made myself scarce for the rest of the day and searched through the brush and woods until it was time to head back to Springfield. I jumped three more deer out of their beds and re-fired my desire to become a woodsman and more particularly, a deer hunter.

My first experience hunting whitetail deer was obviously a memorable and important one for me. I gained some deer stories to tell my friends and family. I saw seven deer and got hooked on deer hunting, and, I became an outlaw. This was the first time I had hunted without a proper permit. I was disappointed in myself, realizing I could so easily throw out my conservation and Christian convictions just to fit in. I discovered I had a lot to learn about being a woodsman.

Chapter 3

1974: Blind Curves in the Dark

Things were going well back at school after the 1973 deer season but I was homesick and confused. My class load and work schedule were fine and my grades were good but I thought there must be an easier way. While at S of O I had joined the campus fire department. The challenge of the work really drew me. It seemed vital and it was much more interesting and exciting than music theory. I began to think a career as a firefighter would be more fitting for me.

I sang lead for the Wiseman Singers; a Southern style gospel group started at Northwest Baptist Church during my senior year in high school. Being a part of the group was very important to me then. However, weekend singing engagements and trips every Thursday back to Springfield to record a local television program took its toll on my resolve to remain in school. I didn't want to give up those weekly trips because they were another opportunity to see Kathy, who I had proposed to by that time.

I dropped out of college in January of 1974. Actually, I transferred to Southwest Missouri State College in Springfield where all the classes I wanted were full so I ended up with just one night class. I was too young to pursue a career as a firefighter so instead, I joined the Cedarbrook Volunteer Fire Department which operated east of Springfield in Greene County. Cedarbrook VFD was a group of five men who built and operated their own fire trucks because there was no Fire Protection District for the county in those days.

It was during this period I took my first paid church job as Music Director for Glidewell Baptist Church. I worked several other temporary jobs until landing at the Ozark Grocer Warehouse late in the spring. My pay was a whopping $2.10 per hour—the minimum wage had just been raised.

Kathy and I were married on July 4, 1974. Getting married on the holiday was the only way we could get a few days off and still be back to church by Sunday. We could not afford to lose the $35 from my music job. I began this special day (with Kathy's blessing) by fishing in a small lake owned by one of the church members. David Davis was my best man. He went with me on the outing because he felt it was his duty even though he wasn't much into fishing. Fishing was about the most relaxing exercise I could imagine at the time and I needed to relax.

The wedding took place mid-afternoon. I arrived at the church and entered the sanctuary on my way to the assigned dressing room, and there was Kathy, who proceeded to scold me for being there, in that particular place, at that particular moment. She said I was jinxing us and my comment about how perhaps she should wear a bell didn't go over well. Her mother then started in on me about why I had not put up the rented canopies and awnings for the outdoor reception. It was the first I'd heard about it, and I was not happy. Actually I was angry but I went to work.

There were no instructions for assembling those particular contraptions and I was melting down in the 95 degree heat in more ways than one. I finally finished putting them together and found a cooler room in the church, out of the bride's way, and began to simmer down. I was still steamed Kathy did not want me to sing to her during our wedding but I guess it just wasn't done in those days. Looking back I can see a long list of personhood issues working on a very young man's mind.

All my anger was quickly quenched though when I saw my beautiful bride walk down the aisle on her father's arm. Everything went fine from there. Except for the fireworks set off outside the sanctuary door, and maybe I should mention the toothpaste that faded the yellow paint, and candy corn melted into the cloth seats of our 1968 Mercury Montclair?

Or should I confess I stopped to fight a brush fire on the way to Branson, and I didn't think it was a problem to go bass fishing from the banks of Tablerock Lake on the second afternoon of our mini-honeymoon? I described in detail what techniques and bait I was using; Kathy was not impressed. I had a lot to learn.

Our first year of marriage was difficult in many ways. We were very young and unprepared for married life. I was foolish enough to assume my cute little wife would gladly tag along and easily fit into my crowded life as a warehouseman, firefighter, choir director, gospel singer, softball player, fisherman, and Would-be Woodsman. Not only was I foolish—I was unfair to assume such.

From my perspective, an extra benefit of being married to Kathy was being a part of her family which meant deer hunting in November. During the fall I hunted with Max and Kathy's brothers, Jeff and Greg. We stayed in Max's Idletime camper at Uncle Bill's place near Dora, Missouri. I may have seen one fleeing deer during the whole trip but my most vivid memory of this, my second deer season, had nothing to do with deer.

Kathy's brother, Jeff, worked at a movie theater in Springfield. I had a Friday night singing somewhere and rode—down home—with him after he got off work around midnight. His mid-sixties Ford Mustang was pretty cool. I slept most of the way, until I awakened somewhere along Highway 14 to discover Jeff was crossing the center line on every one of the many left hand curves. I expressed my brotherly concern. Okay, maybe I yelled at him, something about being an idiot. He basically told me to mind my own business. I told him I thought my life was my own business. He said it was perfectly safe because he would see the headlights of approaching cars as they hurtled through the dark night on the treacherous curves—it was no big deal. I stayed awake and somehow survived the first year of marriage.

Chapter 4

1975: First Harvest
(Confessions of a Poacher)

1975 brought some changes for us. Just before our first anniversary we decided to stay together after a pretty rough year, relationship-wise. We had managed to save a little bit of money and took my one week vacation around the Fourth of July holiday in several parts.

The first phase was to spend one night in Eureka Springs, Arkansas, and take in the Great Passion Play. Kathy had made a reservation at a small cottage court west of the town. We left Springfield after work and arrived at the motel to find it looking run down and scary. There were holes in the screen doors and we didn't see any air conditioning. I turned to Kathy and she gave me an apologetic look and said she did not want to stay there.

We started east on Highway 62 looking for a room but there was no room in the inn—any of them. "No Vacancy" signs were what we found all the way past Green Forest. We even tried a side trip to a little town which turned out not to be a town. The only thing at the *town* was an old and rickety wooden bridge. Our 1970 Mercury barely fit on the two by four treads and I thought I felt the bridge groan and shudder under the weight of our huge vehicle. This place was nowhere. Re-crossing the bridge was the only dreaded alternative if we wanted to return to civilization. As "Dueling Banjos" played in my head I guided my Mercury across the bridge and out of there.

Discouraged and desperate we finally made it back to the highway. We were running out of options and daylight. We had passed a place on our way out of town whose sign said they catered to bus groups. Kathy suggested we pull in and check out Keller's Country Dorm. They had room for us because the holiday weekend was a slow one for groups.

We were relieved and excited until we saw our room. It was a cubicle with two sets of bunk beds. I describe it as a cubicle because the walls were partitions, open at the floor and ceiling. So much for the private, romantic getaway. The rose and bud vase I had sneaked along made the trip better than I did and looked a little out of place in our spartan accommodations. To top it all off, before we could leave for dinner and the Great Passion Play, I had to change a flat on the Mercury.

This trip made quite a healing memory for us. It drew us closer in ways I still don't understand. As we traveled home the next day I realized some things had to change for us to have a chance. To make more space for us I planned to quit the Wiseman Singers. I also realized the pursuit of firefighting as a hobby was expensive, both financially and relationally, but I was reluctant to give it up. Firefighting as a career seemed a distant hope because you had to be 21 years old to fight fire for the city of Springfield. Time seems to move so slowly when you are young.

Kathy and I worked with her mother in the Red Cross first aid booth at the fair later during the summer. The armed forces recruiters were located near our station. The Army recruiter worked me pretty hard. I told him of my plans to pursue a firefighting career as soon as I turned 21. He informed me the Army had firefighters and I did not have to wait until I was 21. I told him I would think about it. After talking about it with Kathy and visiting with a man at work whose brother was a fire fighter in the Air Force I decided to contact an Air Force recruiter.

Things happened fast. I tested well and took a bus trip to Kansas City, Missouri for a physical. Everything was fine except I was four pounds over the weight limit for my height. I came home somewhat disappointed and embarrassed and put the whole idea out of my mind for a while.

It turned out to be a short while. A few weeks later in September I was laid off from my warehouse job so I quickly lost ten pounds and contacted my recruiter. On my second trip to Kansas City, the 26th of September, I enlisted in the United States Air Force with a guaranteed contract for Fire Protection Specialist School. The job was guaranteed only if I made it through basic training on time. My delayed entry date was January 2, 1976. This left me with a couple of months on my hands which I filled with odd jobs and deer hunting.

First Buck

My third season as the Would-be Woodsman was exceptional. Kathy made the trip with me to her aunt and uncle's farm in Ozark County. Max stayed with Grandma Sanders and hunted on the Sycamore side of the creek. On the second morning he made a great 150 yard shot with his Marlin 30-30 on a really beautiful eight pointer.

It seems I was assigned to Kathy's cousin, Clyde, who took me to the Maynard Hill on opening morning. The Maynard Hill was about 80 acres of hilltop and holler with a 15 acre hay field on the upper end. The field might have been 100 yards wide at the west end and sloped down to a narrow but blunt point to the east. Hardwoods and sumac bordered the north side with pines to the south.

Clyde and his friend Homer, a locally famous slayer of deer, sent me to the far end of the field and recommended I find a pine tree and climb it, in the dark. As I slowly made my way down the hillside slope with my trusty 303 British the sky began to lighten. I had purchased the rifle from an older man at work for twenty five dollars. I really had no reason to trust this firearm because I could not afford to shoot it much for practice. Shells were 14 bucks for a box of 20, which was a lot of money on our budget.

As I approached the end of the field in the increasing daylight I spied a cluster of pine trees and assumed they were the trees I was looking for. As I moved slowly toward the trees I heard something walking in the woods to my right. I stopped in the field edge and soon could distinguish a four-legged something as it approached the very tree I meant to climb. The critter, which I assumed was a deer, stopped right under the tree at the edge of the field. I had already released the safety and faced a dilemma.

The desire to fire at the animal was almost uncontrollable. I had a tag. Any deer was legal the first two days of the season. I was 99% sure the animal was a deer but the pine branches covered all but its legs and underbelly. But I could not, for certain, identify the creature.

How thoughts go through your mind at times like this is amazing. I thought about my mother's cousin in Idaho I had never met because his friend fired at something in the brush. I imagined what it would cost me in embarrassment and dollars if I killed someone's calf. My experience identifying deer in the woods was very limited. I waited to see if the probable deer would step out of the cover.

I didn't have to wait long. The deer, oh yes, discovered me standing 30 yards away and decided he didn't want to play. He exploded back into the woods, snorting loudly for several minutes. I did not see antlers. The assumption the deer was a buck was based on the old woods tale that only bucks snort. A professor of later years shared a bit of wisdom: "It is only safe to assume two things; God loves you and it's never too soon for another breath mint." Too true!

So much for the opening morning of deer season. I test climbed a couple of pine trees and finally found a spot suited to me. It was a lovely morning when the sun rose but I did not see any other deer. When I met Clyde and Homer back at the truck they asked if I had seen anything.

Now I have never been good at lies, even little ones, so I didn't try. I told them everything, even the part about thinking the deer could have been a calf. They had a good laugh at my expense. According to these more experienced hunters I should have shot through the tree limbs since any deer was legal the first two days of the season. They would have done more than laugh at me if I had killed a calf.

Later during the morning Clyde and Homer organized a drive and were going to try to run some deer up over the Maynard Hill where I had been posted earlier. They told me to go back and climb the same tree and wait. I had a nagging suspicion their plan was to get me out of the way. It was not fair of me because it turned out to be a hot spot.

I had never been part of a deer drive before so I was interested and excited to say the least. Several of my wife's cousins, their neighbors, and kin were spread out along a ridge top as we guarded some small drains and several avenues of escape. Another bunch of cousins and neighbors made their way toward us from the Billy Mack place, another piece of family land to the north of the Maynard Hill.

I settled in to my chosen pine tree perch with my 303 and waited for whatever. As I leaned back on a limb and enjoyed the sunlight and the bright blue November sky, I began to hear barking and sat up to listen. Yeah, I thought it was barking. Those folks on the drive sounded an awful lot like hounds to me and being the city kid, I was impressed. I knew I had to be mistaken because hunting deer with dogs was illegal in Missouri.

After a while the barks and the human hoots drew closer but they were still down in the holler. Suddenly, a deer stood where the field and woods met about 75 yards directly to my front. I really got excited, as you might expect from a young hunter. I raised my rifle, centered the peep site and post on the deer's body then squeezed off a shot. She just looked confused and ran out into the field a few feet then looked back the way she had come. By then I had another round in the chamber and didn't hesitate to throw it her way. My old gun had a ten round clip and with one in the chamber I had plenty to spare—I thought.

I continued my barrage and grew more frustrated with every shot because she wouldn't fall down like she was supposed to. She would run a few yards and I would shoot. She would run a few more yards and I would shoot again. She kept looking back.

When she had covered about half of the open field her yearling ran out of the woods behind her. I was some panicked about what to do so I shot a few times at that deer as well. All I managed to do was split them up. The doe made it across and disappeared in the woods on the south side. The yearling made it back into the woods on the north.

Like an automaton, I got my shooting thing on and just couldn't stop until the clip was empty. Work the bolt, jerk the trigger, miss then do it again. However, I did notice somehow in the back of my mind, my last few shots struck the ground high upslope over the back of the deer. The evidence was dirt clods jumping up in the air.

I remember thinking it was not right and not fair because I was holding right on the deer. Needless to say, my barrel was hot, but not half as hot as my ears when we gathered to regroup.

Someone said, "Who's the idiot doin' all the shootin'?" One cousin said she had shot four times. It did not satisfy the inquisitor so I confessed once again. "I shot eleven times at a doe and young one". "Did you hit anything?" "No," I sheepishly replied.

After quite a bit of deserved ridicule we helped one of the hunters locate a nice nine pointer he had shot at but thought he missed. One of the dogs was baying way down in the bottom of the holler. We found him standing over the buck and I was glad for the distraction from my huge mistake. As hard as they were on me, I'm glad they were not a shirt tail cutting crew. I would not have had enough shirt left to blow my nose on.

We ate lunch back at the farmhouse and made a couple more drives in the early afternoon. When it came time to set up on stands for the evening hunt everyone told where they were going to be. I naively asked if anyone wanted to go back to the Maynard Hill with me. They gave me the horse laugh and agreed I had scared all of those deer out of Ozark County.

I borrowed one of the farm trucks and returned to the Maynard Hill alone. It was a short but troubling trip back to my selected pine tree. I settled in to watch and think. As I replayed the morning's activities through my mind I recalled the vague picture of the bullets digging dirt up the slope from where I aimed at the deer.

I sat there in the tree and studied my rifle and considered the peep sights. There were two to select with a flip of the thumb. Each had a number stamped into the metal. One read 300 and the other 600. I continued to ponder over just what those numbers meant. Yards maybe? No, it was a European made firearm, it had to be meters. How far was 300 meters? Three football fields, even more! I was on to something important.

I did not know much about ballistics and trajectories but I supposed (which is different than assumed) a 180 grain bullet would have to be lobbed pretty high to shoot that far and at 75 yards, it would probably strike well above the point I was aiming at. Maybe I wasn't such a terrible marksman. Mystery solved.

Around 4:15 I noticed a deer on the far side of the field a couple hundred yards up toward the top. I aimed my not so trusty anymore 303 British and tried my very Daniel Boone best to shoot the deer. It hopped back into the brush after I fired. Needless to say, by now, confidence in my marksmanship was running low. I held a brief conference with myself and decided I had probably not hit the deer but would check on the way out of the field near dark.

About the time I finished my self-to-self conference I saw a deer (it looked like the same one) sneaking down the hill just in the edge of the brush. It looked a lot like the small deer I had forced back to the north side of the hill earlier in the day. As it reached the spot where the deer had exited the woods that morning, I made a quick ballistics decision and chose to aim at a point about midway between the deer's front and rear feet.

Again, I tried my very Daniel Boone best to shoot my first deer, a doe. I could tell by now. After I shot it staggered a little and started to make a bee-line across the open field toward my tree. It stopped about 30 yards away and then fell over.

My heart hammered hard. My breath was quick and shallow. The deer struggled with dying. I could tell I had gut shot it. The deer tried to get up but fell back each time it made the effort. I was upset at the scene and wanted to put the deer out of its misery so I hurriedly cycled another round and shot at the deer. I missed to the left, evidenced by another dirt geyser. Another shot and a miss to the right. I slid down the tree and made my way to the deer. The Would-be Woodsman was nearly out of ammo.

I was panicked and sick over its struggle to die. Taking out the knife my father had sent with me I tried to cut its throat and end its battle. The knife was so dull it would not cut through the hide. Not knowing whether to laugh with joy for my success or cry in sympathy with the dying animal, I did both. Mercifully, for me, the deer died before I had a chance to decide what to do next.

Since my knife was not sharp enough and I did not know how to field dress a deer anyway, I decided just to take my deer back to the farmhouse as quickly as possible. As I ran to get the pickup I dropped the knife in the field and couldn't find it. After wasting 15 more minutes of daylight I gave up and went on to the truck

I was careful not to drive across the field where I had lost Dad's dull knife and pulled up right next to my trophy. It surprised me how difficult it was to pick up a little old deer and place it in the truck bed. It was like picking up a giant balloon filled with warm water.

I drove the truck to the head of the field and approached the gate by the lane. Another truck was waiting for me there. It was Uncle Bill and his daughter Katy. They said they were worried because I had not made it back yet. I told them my reason for being tardy, "I killed a doe."

Uncle Bill got out of his truck and looked into the bed of the one I was driving. "So you killed a doe, huh?" he asked. I didn't answer his obviously rhetorical question. "Well Wayne, what's this here between her legs?" I thought he was teasing me as they had been all day but when I looked for myself the first thing I noticed was two velvet covered bumps between the deer's ears.

It is told to this day the glow from my ears could be seen all the way to Gainesville. Male deer parts come in pairs and I had missed them all. I was embarrassed to have been so caught up in the event I was not attentive to the most obvious details. The assume axiom proved to be true once again. The upside was, I had killed my first deer, and it was a buck—my first buck.

First Antlered Buck (Confessions of a Poacher)

After we returned to the farmhouse on Bryant Creek, I asked one of Kathy's cousins to show me how to dress the deer. We hung the deer from a tree limb and I watched closely with wrinkled nose as he disemboweled the carcass. I was puzzled by the act of sprinkling a heavy dose of ground black pepper in the open cavity of the deer. They told me it was to discourage the dogs and flies from bothering it overnight.

I had placed the sticky backed deer tag on the back leg of the deer as required by law. One of the cousins carefully peeled it loose and replaced the paper backing explaining to me there was no need to check a deer, yet.

I went back to the Maynard Hill the next morning, not too serious about hunting. The loss of Dad's dull knife was on my mind and I found it before I left the field to return to the farmhouse for breakfast. It was clearly stated all hunters (my father-in-law excepted) who had already killed deer would become dogs for the drives on the coming day. It sounded fair to me.

After breakfast, just before we left for my drive dog duties, I called my Mom back in Springfield and told her all about my success the day before. I explained that I would have to work the drives for the other hunters and asked if she would be interested in venison if I happened to take another deer.

The phone conversation was strange for me. I was excited and proud about my success. I was excited about the opportunity to continue hunting but in the back of my mind I felt sad and guilty because I was not being true to myself. I was not following the conservation and game laws I had admired in my youth. My Mom has since reminded me I also told her I did not plan to ever shoot another deer unless it was with a camera. Ha!

Kathy's cousin George had killed a nice eight pointer earlier in the morning. So had my father-in-law as I have already mentioned. Max and George prepared to check their deer. I still have a picture of all three of our deer hanging from a tree beside the house. I reapplied the tag and took my deer with them to the check station which was a family owned country store about ten miles away. I remember how proud I was to check my first deer.

I worked hard and performed my dog duties all day. It was Sunday and when it came time for the evening hunt George and I headed back for the Maynard Hill. George climbed a tree at the upper boundary of the field and I climbed my now favorite tree at the lower end.

It was another beautiful afternoon in the Ozarks but I was pretty fidgety in the tree. I climbed higher and found a place where I could lean back on the trunk and a limb about left shoulder high with my right leg fully extended to a lower limb and my left buttock resting on another limb. My left leg was cocked up on the same limb. It's hard to describe and it may not sound so but I was very comfortable—for a while.

Not long after I settled into to my comfortable limb lounge chair I detected a noise to my right where a tractor trail entered the point of the field. Turning my head a little I was able to watch a doe materialize right before my eyes. My heart began to hammer and my mind began to spin—another case of buck fever like the day before. I thought, "What should I do?" I did not have a tag for a doe. Actually, I did not have a tag for anything.

I watched her casually feed her way out into the edge of the field. From time to time she would look back. This was the last hour of the last day of the—any deer—weekend. I could shoot the doe but I had already used my tag. Someone back at the farmhouse had said if I got one, somebody would surely be glad to tag another deer. Those were a couple of mighty big ifs: one, my shooting another deer; two, someone else willing to tag it. I had not enamored myself to Kathy's family so far that weekend. The doe kept looking back.

It seemed someone had said or I had read a buck will always let a doe enter a field before he does. I detected more faint sounds from the trail and was watching as an eight point buck also magically exited the woods. He followed the doe and fed my way. "What should I do?" I thought again. The fact I didn't have a tag had slipped farther into the back of my consciousness. The possibility of not shooting either deer never entered my thoughts. I had already rationalized my way into this situation—being in the woods with a loaded gun and no tag. I was very concerned about what the other hunters and family members would think of me if I did nothing.

As I pondered my dilemma over which deer to shoot, they continued to feed into the edge of the field and worked their way closer. I could have jumped astraddle of either one. Suddenly, I realized I was experiencing a strange sensation—actually, a lack of sensation. My left leg had been propped up for about forty-five minutes and had gone to sleep. I could not feel my toes. Panic set in and my wild imagination conjured up images of me on crutches with a stump where my left leg used to be.

Panic pressed me to a decision. I would shoot the buck and if no one else would tag it I would drive back to Springfield and get my Mom a tag and check the deer in the morning. The decision made, I was now concerned about the deer sensing my presence when I moved. I assumed (foolish concept again) they would bust me at the slightest motion. I decided I would have to shoot quickly after starting to move.

I slid my backside off the limb and set my left foot on the same limb as my right then discovered I could not see the buck through the pine boughs. I pressed down on the limb with my left foot which was very difficult because my leg was anesthetized. I almost lost my balance as I got a glimpse of the buck and pretty much pointed the gun down in his direction and fired. I missed.

The buck didn't look up as I expected but swapped ends and turned back the way he had come. My practice with the bolt action of the previous day paid off as I reloaded quickly. I took careful aim on his neck and fired. He dropped on the spot and the snorting doe ran out in the field and stopped to figure things out.

I tried to climb down but discovered I had very little control over my left leg. I shouted George's name. In a few minutes I could see him running down the hill. He hollered ahead and asked what was the problem was. I explained my predicament and he made a comment about how beautiful the buck was and how dumb I was. He said, "When you hollered after the second shot, I thought you had shot yourself, but I didn't think even you were dumb enough to shoot yourself twice." By the time blood flow was fully restored to my leg and I made it down out of the tree, George had finished field dressing the deer. I was not as dumb as he thought, I thought.

Back at the farmhouse, no one wanted to check my buck even for all of the venison. The only comment I remember was a question about why I had not shot the doe as well. I was not a favored fellow for some strange reason. On to plan B. I called Mom and told her what I had in mind. It was well after dark when we left for home, 100 miles away. As soon as I got to town I picked up my mother and took her to a grocery store which had a sporting goods section She bought a deer tag. I made arrangements to pick her and Dad up at 6:00 the next morning.

We arrived at the farm around 8:30 and I borrowed one of Bill's trucks and took my deer, my Mom, and my Dad to the check station we had used on Sunday morning. Only the store owner and employees had been present when I checked my first deer. When I turned off the highway the first thing I saw was a Missouri Conservation Commission game warden and his vehicle. I was petrified but said, "Mom, you shot the buck on Bill Butler's farm in Ozark County with a 303 British." I felt sickened at the fact I was an outlaw and now I was coaching my mother to lie for me.

Picture this, my mother, all 4'11.5" inches of her getting out of this rusty farm truck in her straight-from-the-city gray polyester slacks and a purple flowered white blouse with black purse and pumps. Her story—though well told—was unconvincing. When asked to pinpoint on the map where the deer was taken, I had to step in and locate Bill's farm for her. Mom said very little, trying hard not to lie. The game warden never said a word. He just stood back with folded arms and doubtful look. I think I saw him shaking his head a little but maybe that was just my guilty conscience and wild imagination.

I returned to Springfield with my Mom and Dad but quickly travelled back to Ozark County to hunt for a few more days. It was not legal to do this—and I shouldn't have—but I wanted to spend some time with Coy. He was father-in-law to one of Kathy's cousins and he exuded woodsmanship. I simply followed him around for two days, listening to everything he said (which wasn't a lot) and watching his every move in the woods. I learned more from him about hunting whitetail deer than I could have absorbed from a library full of books and magazines. He was a gentle but strong teacher.

Let me wrap this long but significant chapter up. I had taken my first buck and told my first lie. Well, not my first lie, but my first one as a woodsman and it sure felt significant. I had rationalized and justified my choices and actions. I was outwardly proud but inwardly ashamed. I had let myself down. I had let my Lord down. I kept those feelings to myself.

Chapter 5

1976: New Life in the United States Air Force

After Basic Training at Lackland Air Force Base in San Antonio, Texas, and Fire Protection Specialist School at Chanute AFB in Rantoul, Illinois, I received my first choice of assignments—Fairchild AFB near Spokane, Washington. Kathy had family on the west coast of Washington and I had some of my mom's family in northern Idaho so it seemed like a good choice. We knew we were a long way from home when we arrived there, pulling a U-Haul trailer behind our 1970 Mercury Marquis.

Kathy cried when she saw the base and realized almost everything, including the Commissary, the Base Exchange, and the bowling alley were in World War II vintage warehouse buildings. I had spent ten weeks in lovely Rantoul so I was not concerned.

Base housing was not a possibility for an airman (E-2, one stripe) so we looked for an apartment in nearby Medical Lake. We found a nice little two bedroom, first-floor apartment and moved in. There were at least five lakes within a short drive and we were just a few minutes from the air base. The town took its name from a couple of the nearby lakes where Native Americans used to drink the healing waters.

We moved in on a Saturday then drove around the small town and looking for a church we could attend the next morning. We visited the First Baptist Church of Medical Lake on our first Sunday. It was a small church with friendly people, most of whom were retired Air Force or active duty. I recognized one of the members as a civilian firefighter who worked at the main station where I was assigned. Gene Bolt became my lifelong friend. Kathy and I agreed discovering a Southern Baptist church so close to our new home was not a coincidence and we joined the church that evening.

My work at the Base Fire Department involved 24-hour shifts. The days between shifts left some time to pursue my outdoor hobbies although we had very little money to squander on them. Many of my fellow firefighters were deer hunters. As the fall of 1976 approached The Would-be Woodsman was desperate to find places to hunt so I was delighted when a couple of the enlisted firefighters invited me to go with them.

On the first hunt, our civilian Assistant Chief, Gerald Rhinehart, let three of us off early so we could travel 30 miles to our hunting spot before daylight. I thought it was pretty cool that Gerry was a serious deer hunter. The first hint I was traveling in questionable company came early in the trip. Larry Moore drove his cobbled together 1969 Suburban over 80 miles per hour on the fog covered highways. The national speed limit was 55 in those dark days. I was relieved when we stopped at a farmhouse where Buddy Miller, the buck sergeant leading this expedition, spoke to the landowner and verified permission for us to hunt.

The farm lay sprawled in and around the Spokane River and included crop fields along the river bottom, as well as pine-covered canyons, hillsides, and ravines. There were both whitetail and mule deer in the area and I was excited because I'd never seen or hunted mule deer before.

We hunted in a beautiful spot overlooking the Spokane River most of the morning. The Spokane Indian Reservation was across the river to the north and east. We finally took a break to find some lunch in a small town we had passed along the way. It was then I received my second wake up call. As we sped along Buddy shouted, "Look, there's a buck layin' down in that field!" Larry said something unrepeatable and made a sharp turn to the left, crossed the oncoming lane and vaulted the culvert at full speed. My frantic and too late search for the seat belt left me flopping around the backseat like a rescue dummy.

Even in our excitement, flying across the wheat stubble field, we all noticed the buck wasn't moving. We got a little bit closer and saw why—it was actually a dead tree limb sticking majestically out of an uncultivated island in the field. More unrepeatable comments were made. I decided to keep my concerns, doubts, and anger to myself because I was a long way from the house—too far to walk.

During the afternoon we hunted away from the river behind the main farmhouse. I had never before, nor ever since hunted in such a place. There were hundreds, maybe thousands of acres of harvested wheat fields surrounding the farmstead. As I followed Buddy and Larry on a path heading beyond the outbuildings I looked around but didn't think there could be any place to hunt out in these fields. I saw a few pine trees but they didn't inspire much hope.

As we approached those pine trees I realized there was a good sized hole in the ground filled with trees and brush. The closer I got the more impressed I was with hole that turned out to be a canyon. We followed a trail down into the canyon and stumbled around to eventually discover an old homestead at the very bottom, complete with an overgrown apple orchard.

I had read somewhere deer liked apples and was disappointed when Buddy sent Larry and me back to the head of the canyon and told us to hunt along the rim. I have no idea where he went. I had pulled most of a 0400 to 0600 alarm watch and by now was getting tired. As we walked along the eastern rim of the canyon I thought to myself this way of hunting was never going to work. We paused to rest for a few minutes. My heart rate instantly doubled when I discovered a doe standing in the open, facing down the canyon about half way up the opposite side.

I excitedly pointed her out to Larry. Neither of us had a permit to take a doe but Larry insisted she was a buck and he could see spikes. I carried a borrowed, beat-up pair of field glasses and tried to dissuade him. The distance across the canyon was deceptive. His hunting rifle was a Marlin 30-30 with open sights and he began to fire, holding high because of the perceived distance.

As he fired multiple rounds I watched little puffs of dust erupt well upslope from the deer. Definitely a doe, she began to work her way deeper into the canyon and further up the slope. I almost choked when she reached a clump of bull pines where another small feeder canyon joined the main one. A huge buck with a giant rack stepped out into the open. I immediately decided it was time to enter the fray. My firearm was the infamous 303 British.

It would be a long shot and I knew I would need some help. I frantically looked for a rest to fire from and found an old wooden fence post at the edge of the wheat field. As I leaned on it to line up for the shot it snapped over and rolled down the slope. I was not able to locate any other rest so I sat down and tried to set my elbow on my knee but the grade was too steep and my arms and legs too short for that particular trick. Time was running out so I fired one round offhand and saw the dust puff rise up beneath the buck. He reared up on his hind legs like the Lone Ranger on Silver and took off up the feeder canyon. I threw one more desperate shot his way.

At some point Larry had stopped firing his rifle. As I sat there in deep despair he went on and on about what a great shot I had made but it didn't seem so great to me; I had obviously missed. As we headed back toward home I was glad to have discovered a new hunting place but I was sure concerned about the company I was keeping.

I made several more hunts in this area with my firehouse mates but don't remember too much about them now. I do remember discovering combat boots were not warm enough for hunting in cold weather in eastern Washington, and I should be choosier about with whom I hunt.

This piece of knowledge came as a final straw one morning as four of us were traveling in Buddy's Mustang II. We had just turned north on a state highway when Larry spotted a cock pheasant on the gravel shoulder of the road. Buddy backed up and shouted for someone to roll a window down and shoot the bird. What a nightmare. I do not remember if anyone fired. Like a turtle I drew back into my mental shell, praying for protection from my poor choices and promising I would never hunt with these guys again.

I mentioned Gene Bolt earlier. By the end of 1976 I was working for him on our days off. Gene was a framing contractor on the side and would hire several firefighters to work with him from time to time. Before I met Gene I had no confidence about working with my hands. I had told someone once I could not drive a nail straight. Gene taught me how to do that and much more. He taught me how to work. His mantra was, "If it's worth doin', it's worth doin' right." At the end of each long day on a worksite he would pull the old blue Ford away from the job and stop—preferably up a hill. We would get out and view the visual fruits of our labor. We would feel pride and simple satisfaction that we were men and we had worked hard and it looked good.

Many years have passed since I last saw Gene but I think of him every day. My life in the ministry does not often allow me to step back and see what I have done. I find working with my hands and seeing the results—especially building something—is good for my soul. With every project I tackle I ask myself, "Would Gene Bolt do it this way? Would he be proud of me?" I'm proud to call him my lifelong friend and hope he knows.

Chapter 6

1977: New Life in the Family

We discovered Kathy was pregnant right about the beginning of the new year. The winter was a busy one. She worked for H&R Block through the tax season and hated it. I stayed busy working and taking classes in Fire Science at Spokane Community College.

In all my spare time during the winter, when it was too cold to work with Gene Bolt, I decided to improve the looks of my 303 British rifle. I purchased a Birchwood Casey refinishing kit, after some scrimping and scraping, and began to work on my gun. It had already been *sporterized* when I bought it but the wood finish was pretty sad and the bluing of the barrel and action was almost nonexistent.

The stock and fore end finished up real nice but I made a terrible mistake with the re-bluing. An early step in the process is to totally degrease the barrel and action. After applying the degreaser compound I absentmindedly forced the safety and broke the flat metal spring which made the mechanism work. I had no idea where to find a replacement part for my antique firearm but it didn't matter—we didn't have a dime to spend on it. I studied diligently to come up with an alternative.

Eventually I did come up with what I thought was a bright idea. I discovered you could grip the back end of the locked Mauser bolt action between your finger and thumb, apply pressure to the trigger and release tension on the firing mechanism by easing it forward. That process seemed to render the firearm safe. I also discovered I could disable the firing mechanism by leaving the bolt unlocked. We will get back to this brilliant idea later.

During the spring Kathy decided it would be better for us to be living on base when the baby came. I still wore only two stripes and was not qualified to move directly into non-commissioned officer housing. To be eligible for housing on base an airman or airman first class had to be living in the off-base airman housing unit downtown in Spokane. The housing unit was called Garden Springs, not because it was a lovely place, but because it was down the street from the Spokane Arboretum. These one and two bedroom bungalows had been officer housing back during World War II and they were considered substandard because they had only one door.

Kathy and I decided to make the move quickly so we could get on the list to hopefully be assigned a duplex on base before our baby arrived. We rented a U-Haul truck and moved ourselves, with help from our church friends. The move was a low budget affair but I remember how impressed I was with Kathy's ability to fix up the little place on a shoestring.

One of the civilian firefighters was willing to pick me up on his way to work and I really appreciated it since we only had the one car. We had lived in Garden Springs for one week when I received a call at work from the housing office. They wanted me to come by and then go choose between two available three-bedroom duplex houses. We had originally been told it would take several months. I checked them over and talked to Kathy by phone. She was so tired from our move she almost cried at the thought of moving again.

I went back and thanked the nice ladies at the housing office and told them I was afraid Kathy was not up to another move so soon. When I asked them how long they thought it would take to get on base if I placed my name exclusively on the list for a three-bedroom with a garage they said it should happen well before our baby was due so that's how we left it.

Another call came for me on my next shift with news our three-bedroom duplex with full basement and detached garage was available. They also informed me since I was already in military housing the

Air Force would pay for a moving company to pack up and move our things. That swung the deal for Kathy and we made the move. I never found out for sure, but I suspect my civilian boss, Chief Strang, had pulled some strings at the base housing office.

When we moved onto Fairchild Air Force Base our rent was still current in our apartment in Medical Lake and we had to pay an additional fifty dollars for the short time in Garden Springs. So technically, we paid rent on three residences at once. Kathy and I are glad we have never come close to breaking this record. It was nice to have Kathy nearby while I worked 24-hour shifts at the fire department. We were literally minutes away from the base hospital. One of the best things about moving onto base was living near our good friends Paul and Jayne Roberts. Though the assignments, years, and miles would separate us they would always remain dear to our hearts.

We bought a mattress and boxed spring set from Buddy Miller soon after moving on base and somehow I wangled the deal to include a Bear take-down recurve bow and some aluminum arrows. I had wanted to learn to bow hunt and this seemed like a step in the right direction. There was an archery club on base and the commander provided them a place behind the B-52 alert pad for a makeshift range. I practiced there and in the back yard as often as I could until I accidently broke a fellow airman's Arkansas whetstone and ended up trading the bow to set things straight. There would be no archery hunting for me in 1977.

I had better things to do than bow hunt in September of 1977. My fire science curriculum at the community college included the Emergency Medical Technician course. I really enjoyed the course, especially the section on child birth. Our baby was two weeks overdue and I was ready even if she wasn't. Kathy had been ready for a long time.

Kathy was admitted to the obstetrics ward on the morning of September 29 at the base hospital. She received an IV drip to induce labor all day. In addition to labor contractions for 14 hours she experienced seizures due to toxemia. Late in the day her doctor told me his plan. He and I were going to a staff lounge area to watch the Ali vs. Shavers fight. If Kathy had not progressed by the end of the match, he would call in his C team. Not the third string, I was relieved to learn, but the Caesarian section team. I don't remember much about the fight.

I had been pumped up, educated, and prepared to stay right by Kathy's side for a normal delivery but I must admit I was relieved to learn it was against Air Force policy for fathers to observe a C-Section operation. I had no desire to see the surgery if it involved my wife and baby.

A friend of ours from church had a job cleaning the operating rooms. After I kissed my Kathy and prayed, he took me back to an office adjacent to the room where the action would take place. As we were chatting about I don't remember what, I heard a baby cry. I grinned at my friend and said, "It's a girl." Amy Michelle West had finally made her appearance. She was beautiful—the perfect baby.

When I saw Kathy she was pretty groggy still so I told her how proud I was of her and headed home to make phone calls. As I drove the old Mercury off the hospital parking lot my heart was full and my mind was racing. The reality of my fatherhood and new responsibilities were wonderfully overwhelming. By the time I reached our house I could not recall what my life was like before I had a daughter—and it fit me just fine.

Later in the morning I drove the back way into Spokane to buy donuts for the obstetrics staff and my fellow firefighters (instead of cigars). I nearly ran over a doe deer crossing the road. The near collision reminded me firearm deer season was approaching.

I hunted mostly by myself in public areas and on the farm in the Spokane River breaks. I saw a few deer but always after they had seen me. Two of Kathy's cousins came to visit us from western Washington. They brought gifts for Amy and wanted me to take them hunting.

They were really nice fellows and I liked them but they were nearly as outlaw minded as Buddy and Larry when it came to deer hunting. On our way to hunt the Spokane breaks they would have gladly shot a spike buck from the state highway on land we did not have permission to hunt. I had to talk fast but I bluffed them out of their plan to brazenly poach.

Another thing which bothered me was their desire to hunt on

the move at a brisk pace. I saw no future in the tactic so I let the two brothers do their thing while I set up with my back to a harvested wheat field looking down a steep grade to another river bottom wheat field. It sounded like thousands of Canada geese were feeding down there.

This is when my brilliant idea regarding my 303 British rifle proved not to be so. The morning fog was just beginning to lift when I heard a noise behind me. I turned and saw a mule deer run pogo stick-like across the cut wheat field. Moving quickly, I tried to identify gender and get on line for a shot. It was a hopeless situation but it sure got my heart rate up.

I held my rifle in a cradle carry as I made my way back to the stump I had been warming. I walked slowly, eyes on the brush down the slope. Just as my left foot landed in a slight depression I heard a gunshot—close—off to my right. I immediately thought of Kathy's cousins and snapped my head in the direction they had taken. Something was wrong. My rifle was gone. I turned my head back to the left just in time to see the butt of the rifle hit the ground and begin a slow-motion cartwheel. Sick does not begin to describe how I felt.

Trembling, I retrieved the rifle and checked for a barrel obstruction—pondering what had just happened. I did not remember taking the gun off safe when I moved to see the bounding deer, but I obviously had. The old corduroy coat I wore had large toggle buttons. One of the buttons must have hung in the trigger guard and discharged the firearm when I stepped hard into the hole.

I prayed and thanked God no one had stood near me when I committed such a foolish act. I prayed no one had been hurt by the errant bullet I had sent across the river onto the Spokane Indian reservation. I prayed for forgiveness of my carelessness. Sharing this confession, even now, triggers a shudder deep down in my soul and a heartfelt prayer of thanksgiving.

The Would-be Woodsman learned a valuable lesson. No matter how badly you want to be in the field, never hunt with equipment that does not function as designed. Take no short cuts when it comes to safety. The latter part of this lesson is still a challenge for me.

13 Point Buck

It was very unusual for a two striper (airman first class) to be chosen to attend an advanced course at the Air Force Fire Protection School back in beautiful Rantoul, Illinois. I imagine the fact I was one of the few military firefighters who did not smoke dope on their day off had something to do with it. I was chosen to attend the two-week Fire Protection Systems course in December of 1977.

It worked out perfectly. I was allowed a thirty day leave in conjunction with the school which would allow Kathy six weeks at home with her family, showing off our beautiful baby. It also would allow me to return to the Maynard Hill to hunt whitetail deer. We flew home just a few days before the season began. I think I was more excited about hunting than being home. It worked out perfectly.

I know I have said that already but it was true. The opening morning of deer season found me on the Maynard Hill with my father-in-law, Max. He graciously allowed me to hunt with his Marlin 30-30. I climbed my pine tree and he moved into the woods below the point of the field. A doe ran between us but we were kind to each other and did not shoot. Nothing memorable happened the rest of the day.

The next morning things were quite different. Max had chosen to hunt somewhere else. I remember that particular Sunday morning very clearly. It was unusual for me to be hunting on a Sunday morning. It was a beautiful, cold, frost-covered-everything morning. The kind of morning you read about in Outdoor Life or Sports Afield. Frozen leaves released small explosions with every step I took on my way to the tree.

I made it back to my pine tree in the dark. I knew the way well. Bundled in several layers of clothes, I perched like a fat squirrel on my favorite limb. As it grew light I heard dogs sounding far down the holler to the east. I wondered if they chased a deer. The barks and howls faded out only to be replaced by the sounds of something bounding in the frosted leaves. I could not see anything yet but every explosion seemed closer. My heart rate increased proportionately. I knew it had to be a deer.

Does were legal but you know I hoped it was a buck. Suddenly, the sound stopped and there at the edge of the field about 75 yards away, I could see a deer. It was impossible to make out any headgear due to the backdrop of wild plum.

It seemed to be a large-bodied deer. I had Max's ancient and heavy 10 X 50 binoculars hung around my neck. The rifle rested on a pine bough and with one hand I slowly brought the binoculars up to my eyes. The wind shifted around to my back as I raised the binoculars. I started to panic as I imagined my scent being blown straight toward the deer. It wasn't just my wild imagination this time. Before I could get the glasses focused the buck's head swung up sharply and he looked in my direction. He had winded me.

That's right—definitely a buck! How much buck I still didn't know but it was time to stop thinking and get into action. I brought the rifle up quickly and rested it slightly on a pine limb as I squeezed of my Daniel Boone best shot just as the deer spun back toward the woods. The tail went down and I thought I could see the deer fall as it disappeared.

I slid down out of the tree like it was a brass pole in a fire station then sprinted the 75 yards to where I had last seen the deer. To this day I don't know why I did it but all along the way I peeled off layers of clothing. I threw off my hat. I pulled off my gloves. I evaded my vest. I cast off my coat. If it had been any further I might have been buck naked when I arrived at the deer.

Oh man! He looked like a true monarch of the forest. His rack was so tall and beautiful. I could not believe I had made a tough shot on such a trophy animal. I awoke from my splenderous daydream when I realized the king of the woods was trying to get up. I was not about to let him escape so I shot him again and he quickly died.

I was shaking; more than when I shot my first antlered buck—even more than when I had killed the button buck. I was in such a state I almost fell down. I was also cold and began to retrieve my wardrobe. The big buck was hard to move into position for field dressing. It was huge and I was worthless weak.

I knew Homer the Deerslayer was hunting for this very deer not too far away. Making my way to his ambushment I asked him if he would come and help me. He said, "Did you kill my deer?" I replied, "Yeah

Homer, I think I did." He came back, "How big is it?" I said, "Well, it's got at least ten. You might count more. He expressed an explicative which I cannot share here. I know he was disappointed and angry. Neophyte nimrods from the city are not supposed to kill the best bucks. It's just not right. Yet he helped me field dress the trophy and load it in the back of Max's pickup. I have always appreciated his willingness to help me with a chore which was joy for me and pain for him.

As we grunted and strained to lift the buck in to the truck bed Homer could not resist a parting shot. He said matter-of-factly, "This deer don't weigh a hundred pounds." It was the largest deer checked at Gainesville that day and the biggest seen around those parts for many years. It was recorded as a thirteen point buck.

We returned to Springfield and had the deer processed. Max had hired a man in Seymour to mount his eight pointer in 1975. I arranged with him to do a shoulder mount. The price was $65. I gave him a $19 deposit (all I had) and told him there was no rush since I did not expect to be back to Missouri for quite some time.

I managed to develop pneumonia while at the fire school because I slept in a World War II barracks next to a frost-covered wall with a hot steam pipe about a foot from my face. I was sick all through Christmas back in Springfield and the flight back to Spokane was the most miserable I ever made.

The Would-be Woodsman learned a lot about life and hunting in 1977. Being a father is a wonderful thing. My experiment in the gunsmith craft had led me into an awful mistake which the grace of God had seen me through. I also learned success as a hunter has a lot to do with being in the right place at the right time, with a great dose of help from the Lord.

Chapter 7

1978: A Strange and Troubling Year

A lot would happen to our family in 1978. The core of our life in Washington was anchored in the First Baptist Church of Medical Lake and our wonderful friends there. We experienced a pastor's departure followed by a tumultuous interim period. Our friendships within the church were strong and we found ourselves pulled between a faction of friends from the south who wanted a southern-fried Baptist Church and a group of native westerners who did not care for loud preaching and Southern Baptist traditions. We weathered the storm and our faith grew through the painful process.

Our church called a pastor from northern California early in the summer. I decided I liked him once I discovered he was a bow hunter. I really liked him when he offered to lend me his old compound bow, though I didn't always understand things he said from the pulpit.

A very significant part of this strange year involved our daughter Amy. Kathy brought Amy to the firehouse around suppertime one early summer evening as she often did. She seemed disturbed and Amy was crying. Kathy explained they had just come from the Fairchild Air Force Base Hospital where the staff had examined Amy and found no reason for her crying.

Kathy explained she had been in the kitchen and Amy was walking along holding onto the couch in the living room. She heard her plop down and begin to cry. This was pretty common when Amy was learning to walk but this time the crying didn't stop.

Being an EMT trained fire protection specialist I examined her myself. We went into the Chief's office and used his desk. Amy could not bear weight on the right leg and the intensity of her crying would increase when I touched her hip and thigh. I did not think it was her hip because it did not rotate out. I told Kathy I was pretty sure Amy's femur had been fractured.

I was angry at the pediatricians at the base hospital. They had not even taken an x-ray. Kathy took Amy home and nursed her through a long night. As soon as I got off shift the next morning I took Amy and Kathy back to the hospital. I was as strong and forceful with the commissioned doctors as an airman first class could dare to be. I convinced them an x-ray was needed.

The x-ray clearly revealed a spiral fracture of Amy's femur. I was angry at the doctors for putting Kathy off the day before and was heartsick Amy was hurting. The staff explained there was no orthopedic surgeon currently assigned there for dependents and we would have to take Amy to another hospital downtown. It meant we would have to come up with the deductible for our CHAMPUS insurance.

We were able to see a surgeon in Spokane that afternoon. It was a Friday. After examining Amy he told us he would do surgery on Monday to place Amy in a body cast. The Spica cast would cover from the toes of her broken leg up and around her hips and waist then down below the knee of her good leg. There would be an opening for necessary functions. She would be in the cast for six weeks. Kathy and I were heartbroken as we looked at our suffering baby girl.

It had been a very long, emotional, and physically draining day and it would be a long weekend as we waited for Monday. When we got home I cried for Amy and us. I couldn't help her. We called our families in Missouri and Kathy's parents assured us they would help with the finances and they did. Amy had some medicine to help her with the pain so we were able to settle her down for the night.

I went to bed, an exhausted wreck, and fell into a deep but troubled sleep only to awaken sometime later, confused because Kathy was standing by my side of the bed. She was trying to hand me a folded piece of paper. Still dazed, I took it and she walked out of the room.

The note was an explanation of what really happened to Amy. I came fully awake instantly. It had not happened at our house. Kathy had taken the car downtown to Spokane to shop at KMART. When she was checking out she had set Amy up on the counter right by her while she reached into her purse. Amy had been walking around the furniture at home and had become fearless of falling. She decided to get down. Twisting away from Kathy she fell to the floor, evidently landing on her right knee.

Kathy said she had been embarrassed and had made up the story she told the doctors and me. The note told how sorry she was to have lied because it had prolonged Amy's suffering. If she had told the truth they would have examined her properly. She asked my forgiveness.

I sat on the edge of the bed for a while, not mad, just hurt. God spoke to my heart as I sat there. He reminded me how our marriage had changed since Amy's arrival. I no longer had Kathy to myself and had struggled with the change. We were both brand new at parenting but I had become unfairly critical about her care of Amy and had said some hurtful things. I realized Kathy was not just embarrassed but afraid—of me. I asked God to forgive me.

I found Kathy in the kitchen, held her in my arms, and asked her to forgive me for making her afraid to tell me the truth. I tried to assure her Amy's pain was my fault, not hers. This event was huge and I knew it. I recommitted my life to God, our marriage, and our family.

Six weeks in a body cast made for the longest summer of our young lives. God was gracious and Amy was wonderful. My fire chief found me an eight-hour job so Kathy would not have to care for Amy alone during my 24-hour shifts. God took a tough situation and blessed us through it all. To top it all off, I was selected for an early promotion to E-4 at the end of the summer. After every summer, even hard summers, comes the glorious fall and the Would-be Woodsman was ready.

The bow the pastor had loaned me was a huge contraption—one of the original Bear Whitetail bows. It was about four feet from axle to axle and sported a total of six pulleys. I practiced regularly, shooting at some straw bales I stacked behind the main fire station. The bow was a right handed bow. Since I am mostly right handed I was satisfied. Many years later I discovered I am left eye dominant.

At the pastor's recommendation, I ordered a dozen western cedar arrows and some solid, triple bladed broadheads. I gained confidence as I became consistent at hitting a paper plate at 40 yards. Now, I understand my confidence was unwarranted because my broadheads were never near sharp enough to hunt successfully and ethically. I just didn't get that part yet.

Though I had some close calls during bow season, I never loosed an arrow at a deer. I realize now it was for the best. My skills and equipment would have most likely wounded deer and wasted venison.

One morning in October I was doing the required thorough daily checkout of my assigned firefighting vehicle. One of the senior non-commissioned officers pulled me aside and told me he had seen my name on a set of remote assignment orders to Shemya Air Force Base, Alaska. My heart sank.

This was not supposed to happen. Kathy and I loved our friends and church in Medical Lake. We did not want to leave yet. I was angry at the military injustice of it. Reliable GI rumor held there was supposed to be a rule on the books an airman could not be ordered on a remote assignment within eighteen months of his discharge date. So much for reliable rumors!

I went to the deputy chief's office and asked to see him. He was a really sharp and good senior master sergeant. He verified the rumor. I had orders to report to Elmendorf AFB, Alaska, by December 28 to be processed into the 5073rd Air Base Group, Shemya AFB, Alaska.

Shemya is a two-by-four mile island so far out in the Aleutians the International Date Line detours around it and two neighboring islands just to keep them in the same day as the rest of the United States. It lies 400 nautical miles from the Kamchatka peninsula of Russia and 150 nautical miles from the nearest military occupied Russian Aleutian island. There were several firefighters in the station who had been there. They referred to Shemya as The Rock, which called to mind a famous prison.

I stumbled into the firehouse bunkroom to find my bed in the corner cubicle and sat down hard. My head was spinning. There was a huge lump in my throat. My heart was breaking. Amy would grow so much in a year and I would miss her. What would I do without Kathy? In the midst of my pity party a picture came to my mind of our fairly recent past. Kathy and I had knelt beside our living room couch and prayed together. We told God how we wanted to be His people—nothing held back—wherever He wanted us to be.

Reminded of my promise, I asked God to help me be strong and trust Him. I got up and went to ask the assistant chief for a half hour off to go home and tell Kathy in person. When I got to the house and told Kathy the bad news she looked shocked. Amy was taking a nap. We knew our lives had just taken a new turn as we held each other and cried a little.

As we knelt by our couch to pray again she said, "I'm pretty sure I am pregnant." I told Kathy I didn't want to go and leave her alone with our now two children but I couldn't see resisting this in view of our fresh recommitment to God. She agreed and we began our new journey in prayer.

Things happened fast. When I told my friend Gene about my orders he was visibly upset. Gene told me a couple of days later I did not have to take the assignment. I'm sure I looked puzzled until he explained he had an old friend in personnel who would cancel my orders as a special favor to him. I am still touched by the depth of Gene's friendship. I've never had a friend who wanted to keep me around as much as Gene did.

When I told Gene I didn't think I could accept the offer, he looked like he thought I had lost my mind. I tried to explain to him I did not want to go but could not get away from the thought, "What if God wants me to go to Shemya?" I said, "If God wants to get me out of this assignment, I am perfectly willing for Him to do that. But, Gene, I can't duck it or shove my willful way out of this and still honor my commitment to God. What if I am supposed to go and don't. Maybe the guy who gets the assignment crawls into a bottle out there and destroys his life and family. I can't take the chance. Unless God does something obviously supernatural, I'm going to assume this is His will and I'm on my way to The Rock."

I was able to get in a few days of gun hunting for deer just before we were scheduled to leave. My confidence in the old 303 was completely gone. Herman Joyner, one of the deacons at church, loaned me a sweet little 6.5 Swedish Mauser he had picked up years before through a Sears mail-order catalog. It was a rare military surplus gun. All of the part numbers matched and it was accessorized with a 2.5 power scope.

My name had come up in the drawing for an antlerless deer permit and I tried hard to fill it. I hunted up on the Spokane River breaks again but found no opportunities for a good, safe shot. One of the families in our church ran a cattle operation out west of Medical Lake. My friend offered to take me hunting one morning in the sage hills and rolling pastureland of his place. It was a new kind of hunting for me.

We drove along the dirt trails of the sage hills and stopped occasionally to glass for game. Rod spotted several deer in a distant hayfield and the hunt was on. We hunkered and hustled through the sage brush to get ahead of the mule deer. We were in prone position at the barbed wire fence along the field when they drew even with us about a hundred yards away. Rod said he would shoot the four pointer and then I could shoot a doe. We both were resting our guns on the lowest strand of wire—a bad idea. We both missed.

Three does ran away to the south as the buck moved off to the east. We tracked the does and would catch a glimpse of them from time to time. They did not seem particularly bothered by us. We came to a knoll and Rod suggested we split up and carefully work our way around it. Before we parted Rod said, "Wayne, you've only got a few days left before you leave. We need to fill your doe tag. Is it all right with you, if I have the shot, to take it?" He was older and a more experienced hunter than me so I agreed, immediately wishing I had not.

When I reached the other side of the knoll I saw the three does on another little hill not more than 75 yards away. I took a rest on a pine tree and had one in my sights. Out of the corner of my eye I saw Rod was forward of my position and also taking aim. I wanted to tell him I would take the shot but I did not. He fired and I saw the hit. In foolish frustration I also fired. Thankfully I missed. When Rod asked why I had fired, I had no answer.

On the way back to the truck I was about 50 yards behind Rod. As we made our way through some tall weeds and brush a coyote crossed from right to left between us. Even a road killed coyote was bringing $65 at the Spokane tannery. I saw dollar signs. When the animal saw me she took off like a streak of lightning. When she reached a safe zone, well clear of Rod, I swung the rifle on her and made my best shot ever on running game.

Rod, of course was startled and angry. I was angry at myself for letting Rod fill my tag but felt a little satisfied when I bagged the coyote. I was disappointed to discover the coyote's pelt was ravaged by mange and worthless. I was still proud of the running shot. I know now it was mostly luck.

It was decided Kathy and Amy would stay with her parents in Springfield while I was gone. Kathy did the research and decided we could make a self-move back to Missouri and save some money. Paul and Jayne Roberts graciously hosted us on our last night on Fairchild.

I think it was Halloween afternoon when Kathy and I crawled up into the cab of a 24- foot U-Haul truck with Amy's car seat between us. We left our friends and comfortable life behind.

A snow storm had passed through earlier in the day. We thought about delaying our departure, but you can stand to say good-by just so many times and we all were beyond our limit. Halfway up Lookout Pass on the Idaho-Montana border we had second thoughts. The only thing we could see through the dark, snow-swirling night were the trailer lights of a big rig moving steadily ahead of us. With God's protective guidance and those lights we moved ahead of the storm as we reached Missoula. It was freezing cold there and the fuse to the heater motor had blown. I was able to repair it—thankfully.

We spent a frigid night in a log cabin motel room with one electric space heater. It was so cold in the room the next morning we were not brave enough to shower. The storm had surged on ahead of us in the night and we had to stop mid-morning for a couple of hours while the passes were cleared. We followed the storm across Montana viewing crashed automobiles and jack-knifed trucks all along the way. Our vehicle was governed at 52 miles per hour. God knew what we needed.

One time I felt the truck lose traction as we crested a rise. Using my best emergency vehicle driving skills, and God's help, we moved safely through the hazard. When we cleared the top we saw a tractor and trailer demolished in the median and several crashed cars and vans on the right. I again thanked God for watching out for us.

We found a room in Sheridan, Wyoming, at the end of a long day. Amy, at thirteen months, was not adjusting well to road life. Kathy sat up with her and I got a couple of hours sleep. Amy could not settle down so we decided to get showers and hit the road again. We continued to follow the storm.

We caught up with the snow in southern Wyoming which turned to freezing rain as we approached Denver. I had the bright idea to press on through to western Kansas before calling it a day. When we finally reached Goodland, Kansas, there was no room in the inn—any of them. Nothing was available at the next town either so we pushed on eastward.

The freezing rain eventually let up as we drove on through the night. I was starved for sleep but there was nowhere to stop. Kathy tried to keep me awake but eventually succumbed herself after taking care of Amy non-stop for over 40 hours. I was so tired I could not maintain even the governed speed and eventually settled for about 35 miles per hour. We were on I-70 and I was really glad for two lanes because when my eyes crossed I could drive between the two dotted white lines and stay in the road.

Kathy was asleep and thankfully so was Amy. I was not far from it. At the darkest part of the terribly long and lonely stretch of road I noticed headlights in my side view mirrors. This vehicle did not pass even though I was creeping along at a snail's pace. I do not know how long my escort followed me but those lights in the mirrors helped me focus and stay awake. I'm sure I drifted and swerved but the vehicle stayed close by. We finally came to a rest stop and did both. I will never forget those God-sent lights in the mirror.

Kathy's brother Greg was living just south of Kansas City, Missouri. We arrived at his apartment early in the afternoon. The food and showers were great and a nap would have been a good idea but we were too excited to delay. We were only four hours from home. We thankfully said goodbye to Greg and headed south.

We will always remember the wonderful almost-home feeling we experienced when we began to see the Springfield lights in the sky as we made all 52 miles per hour heading down Highway 13. We arrived weary but intact at the Sanders residence just a few days before the opening of deer season. Was that why I was so anxious to get home? Probably.

I borrowed Max's Winchester 30-30 rifle and his Ford pick-up truck for the trip down home and arrived in Ozark County the Friday before opening day. Uncle Bill took me aside and explained he would like some venison for his winter freezer. He would come and get it and farm tag it. All I had to do was shoot it. Even though it was technically illegal, it seemed reasonable at the time and I told him I would if I could. I scouted around the Maynard Hill and was real excited about the visible deer sign: rubs, scrapes, tracks, and droppings.

My excitement faded when everyone else arrived later in the evening. It seemed a not so favorite brother-in-law of mine was coming to hunt and I was assigned, in no-uncertain-terms, as his guide. He would not get off work until early the next morning and my sister-in-law would drive him down and meet me at the Maynard Hill before daybreak to get him set up.

He was not really a bad guy but listening to him talk was like reading science fiction—unbelievable. He had never been hunting before but spoke as if he were a contributing editor for Field and Stream. The opening morning hunt came and went. The brother-in-law said he'd had a good nap. No one in the group shot a deer. I'm not sure anyone even saw one. They just weren't moving. The mid-day drives did not produce any venison either. Everyone was frustrated.

We returned to the Maynard Hill for the evening hunt. It was a gorgeous day but again the deer were not moving in the fields. The only activity was a small plane flying slow patterns over the Ozarks hills. I had been told this plane was the Missouri Conservation Commission air patrol. I remained perched in my pine tree until the end of legal shooting light. I crossed the lower end of the field where I had killed all of my deer so far and began working my way back up toward the truck.

About half way up the edge I heard crashing in the sumac and cedars on the right. My suspicion it was several deer was verified as a doe ran out into the field. I could hear others heading for the holler where the brother-in-law was supposed to be. I instantly thought, "Uncle Bill's venison!" I shouldered Max's gun and sent a 30-caliber bullet toward a very moving target. That I had connected was doubtful.

I immediately became angry with myself. The visible flame belching from the muzzle reminded me it was well past legal shooting light. There was nothing legal or ethical about this situation which was made worse by the fact my sin was not a secret. The game warden plane buzzed the Maynard Hill right after I shot.

One bad choice usually leads to another. I ran to the crest of the field to see if I could catch sight the doe before she reached the woods. That decision was foolish. I soon gave up and tried to return to the exact spot of the poor shot. I lost my bearings and one of my gloves. I headed for the truck still wondering if I had hit the deer.

Calling out to the brother-in-law when I reached the truck I was puzzled to receive no answer. I was anxious to know if he had seen the deer. They should have run right over him. I called several times before I noticed some stirring in the cab of the truck. My narcoleptic nimrod brother-in-law explained he had been asleep in the truck since 4:00. I was angry at him, but unfairly so. He had not broken any laws or promises—I had.

When we arrived back at the farm house I discovered supper was not quite ready and no one else had seen a deer. I scrounged up a flashlight and headed for the door to go look for the doe and glove. One of the cousins asked me where I was going. I confessed and the next thing I know there were three men and one of their sons in a 1965 salvaged USAF crew cab Dodge pickup on our way back to the scene of the crime.

It just so happened the truck was accessorized with a high powered light beam capable of supporting the weight of a full-grown man on a foggy night. They were planning to use it to check on their cattle. They checked every field—even their neighbors'—as we traveled the gravel road back to the Maynard Hill. It was standard operating procedure in those parts to keep your firearm loaded at all times, especially while driving down a road during deer season. You might see a deer at any time.

The son in the back seat asked his father if he could shoot a rabbit with his 20 gauge shotgun. The dad consented and a suitable specimen was soon spotted and held under light. The teenaged boy slowly opened the door and shot at the rabbit less than five yards away. I think he forgot to switch the slug for shot. The bunny hopped off unscathed but I was getting nervous.

My nervousness became full blown panic when headlights appeared ahead of us immediately following the shot. I quickly ejected all rounds from the magazine of Max's rifle. As I was bent forward picking up ammo the vehicle approached and stopped beside us. It was Homer the Deerslayer and his teenaged son. The word was Homer usually showed up around supper time. He had his coon dogs, hunting cap with light attached, and nearly silent .22. After explanations of my poor shot Homer and his son got in the back seat and we continued our quest.

We moved briefly out on the paved road and Homer said something to the effect that since they were checking for cattle he also would like to shoot a rabbit, but only a young one. We turned off the hard surface and headed down the Maynard Hill lane. Homer lit up a young rabbit by an old hog pen to the left side of the truck and shot it. He got out and was field dressing it when his son shined a flashlight out the right side of the truck. Things got lively when he shouted, "Daddy, there's three bucks!"

I was riding shotgun in the front seat. As I was pushed out the door I went straight to the ground and crawled to the rear of the truck. I knew it would be dangerous to stand up. All the doors flew open and the unique metallic sounds of various rifle actions cycling could easily be heard. Homer said, "Don't shoot boys, somebody's bound to get killed. Let me show you how to do this."

He turned off his cap light, stepped over the four-strand, barbed-wire fence, and eased out into the winter wheat field which, by the way, was owned by a family they were feuding with. The deer had not moved far and Homer located them without the light. When he turned his light on, all three bucks were held under its power. In attendance at this meeting was a mature buck, a six point buck and a button buck. Homer's coon hunting rifle popped and the button fell in its tracks.

Homer and one of the cousins decided they would take care of the deer and the rest of us should go on to the Maynard Hill field and look for my deer and glove. It would serve as a diversion if the landowners were looking. I was mad by this point. This was not in my plan. I had tried to do the right thing and make good effort to recover the deer I had shot at. Things had gotten way out of hand.

The cousin driving had me get in the bed of the truck and direct the light as he drove around the field. We did not see anything but we heard the recovery detail shout, "Turn that (expletive deleted) light out, you can see it in Gainesville!" I complied with the request just in time to see the lights of a small aircraft buzzing the Maynard Hill once again. We assumed it was a game warden.

I had assumed the recovery detail would dress the little buck in the field and we were in no rush. Obviously, I was uneducated in such nocturnal matters and was quickly taken to school about it as they threw the deer into the truck bed. As we started down the lane toward the pavement we saw what looked like a flair shot out of the circling airplane. There was later debate about whether it was actually a flare or a shooting star.

These men had all grown up in these woods and lanes; a fact of which I was glad as we traveled through the dark night without headlights. Internally, I was an emotional wreck. This event felt like times in my childhood where neighborhood friendly evening adventures quickly escalated into dangerous and risky business. I had caved in to peer pressure once again. The idea of shooting a deer for someone else had been a small thing, I thought. That small idea had now grown into something out of control.

I pondered these things until Homer spoke up from the back seat, "Boys, if they catch us I'll tell 'em you had nothing to do with this." I wasn't too comforted. Assessing my situation, I knew I was in deep trouble if we were caught. This offense carried a $500 fine, confiscation of a firearm which wasn't mine, and potentially additional prosecution under the Uniform Code of Military Justice for "Conduct Unbecoming an Airman."

As I was thinking how glad I was we were not in Max's truck, Homer took a deep breath and let out a foul oath which made my already clabbered blood run cold. It went something like, "No I won't! I'll kill 'em before I let them take me alive." He spat it out with convincing venom and plenty of unprintable expletives. I had never heard Homer speak that way before.

My mind chased through the list of my guilt. I had attempted to take a deer I did not hold a permit for, after legal shooting hours. I had become an accomplice to poaching by spotlight on someone else's property and now was about to become an accessory to attempted or perhaps successful murder. Talk about a slippery slope. Yes, I was in very deep trouble.

While our driver eased us along the dark and dusty roads of Ozark County I had a seemingly one-sided conversation with God. It went something like this: "Father, forgive me for not being strong enough to say 'no' to what I knew was wrong for me. I'm in a tight spot here You know, but no matter how it turns out, I promise You if I ever get to hunt again, I will play by the rules or I won't play at all."

The first thing I did when we reached the farm house was lock Max's gun in his truck. Two men took the deer into the woods and hid it after dressing it. The driver and his son drove the truck to the milk barn and washed the blood out of the bed. When we entered the house, guilt and fright must have been all over our faces because the women asked if someone had been shot.

We did not venture out to coon hunt that night but stayed in the house and watched for lights coming down the road. Our hearts stopped several times as cars did come down the gravel road but moved on to the last house on the lane. Speculation was made that, if indeed it was a game warden plane, they were watching for us to move out on the roads toward town, not further into the Ozarks wilderness.

I do not remember hunting any more that season. I probably did but the joy was gone. My mind was elsewhere. It was time to focus on preparations for leaving my family for a year.

One Sunday afternoon during the month before my departure for Alaska I was suffering from cabin fever and several other anxiety disorders. I leapt at the opportunity to make a mad dash to the grocery for diapers. I say—mad—dash because I was mad about something. I don't' remember what, but it was a common emotion for me in those days.

We had sold our car in Washington but Max and Ardelle were always generous with theirs when we needed them. I was driving Max's 1976 Ford Explorer. There was a half-load of firewood on board. On the return trip I was traveling on east Cherry Street at about 35 miles per hour when I approached the overpass to the Highway 65 Bypass. As I entered the bridge I noticed a light colored Ford Maverick signaling its intention to turn left onto the outer road. A voice in my head shouted, "He's going to go!"

I stomped the brakes immediately, pumping madly to control the skid as I felt the load of wood pushing me forward. In the final yards as I approached the intersection I realized there were cars stopped at both sides of the intersection. With nowhere safe to maneuver I braced for the unavoidable impact. I literally stood on the brakes and extended my arms as I gripped the steering wheel.

The front end of the pickup was nosed down as I struck the turning car in the passenger side. The impact lifted the car up on its left side, blowing out both tires and shattering every glass in the vehicle. My crash rescue training took over as both vehicles came to rest.

I was unhurt. That could not be said for Max's truck. A quick move to the car revealed both the driver and passenger were conscious. I asked the passenger if she was injured. She said her leg hurt and I could see moderate bleeding from her right knee. I asked the same of the young driver.

All he would answer was, "Whose fault was it?" I was stunned by his response and answered, "You turned left in front of me." He replied in a louder voice, "But whose fault was it?" I said, "Sir, it's yours." He screamed, exited the vehicle, and ran east on Cherry. I saw him stop about 150 yards away.

My puzzled look moved the young lady to explain to me their date was his first attempt to drive since his license had been revoked two years earlier when he was sixteen. One of the gathering crowd said the police and ambulance were on the way. The young lady went to try and convince the driver to return to the scene.

The man in the vehicle behind me stepped up and said, "I could not believe how fast you got on your brakes." I believed I had benefitted from celestial help and told him so. When he asked if there was anything he could do I asked him to go to my in-law's house and inform them of the accident. As he left he assured me he would return to give the police a statement.

Max quietly showed up and stood by me as I gave my statement to the police. Of course he was not pleased I had wrecked his beautiful truck but he did not say or otherwise communicate anything to me but strong support. He had the truck towed to the dealership where he worked.

Just after Christmas Kathy took me to the Springfield airport. We had decided it would be best to leave Amy at home. Our parting plan was for me to return home on leave in five months for our second child to be born. We exchanged a tender kiss and I boarded the plane with a huge lump in my throat. What a strange and troubling year.

Chapter 8

1979: No Hunting on Shemya

There was snow on the ground, as you might expect, when I arrived at Elmendorf AFB in Anchorage, Alaska. It was cold—nose hair freezing cold. Having a report date between the holidays seemed dumb to me because we could not accomplish any of our processing until the second day of January. I use the nominative plural because I met people who were going home after a year and those who were just arriving like me.

One of those men processing out had been stationed with me at Fairchild. Our meeting disturbed me. He had been a new Christian when I had known him before but it was obvious his remote assignment had been a crisis of faith for him. He stood in the hallway of the transient barracks drinking a beer as he told me how he had survived his miserable experience. He had simply stayed in his room and drank beer when he was not working. He had also gotten huge. I was stunned.

I met Senior Airman Ricky L. Pope, from Dallas, Texas. We hit it off right away. We discovered we had entered the Air Force on the same day; had been herded through same crowded room at 2:30 in the morning to be assigned to our separate training flights; had been on the same chartered flight to tech school at Chanute; and attended the same Fire Protection School but had never met. I was on A Shift and he was on B Shift. It seemed the computer had spit our names out to fill slots out on Shemya. Even then I felt there was more to it.

Ricky and I were inseparable during this in-between time. We hit the base gym, the movie theater, and the Base Chapel. Ricky and I both declined to take communion during our first Protestant Chapel service. As we were walking back to the Mattanuska chow hall (pronounced Mighty-nasty by the GI's) we talked about our reasons. I thought the chaplain had said some weird things and my old pastor had cautioned me about military chaplains. Ricky said he didn't take part because they had called the Lord's Supper communion and he didn't know what that was. Yep, we were both Southern Baptist boys all right.

This was the first of many conversations we would have about the Lord in the coming year. Before we left Anchorage we pledged to encourage each other to grow in Christ and to be faithful to our God and families. We both wanted to become better men. In addition to our spiritual goals we wanted to lose some weight and get in better shape. I also had the lofty goal of improving my penmanship. No one who knows me now will believe it, but it's true. The only piece of that effort to remain is my signature. My wife and daughters still think it is horrible.

We flew out to Shemya on Reeves Aleutian Airways aboard a four engine turbo prop aircraft. My first impression of the Reever was not a good one as I watched the wing tips flap like a bird when the outboard engines fired up. I immediately took pen to paper and wrote Kathy a letter which started, "You may never get this letter. . . ." I also spoke to God as we were waiting to take off and told him if I made it home after this assignment I would be satisfied to stay on the ground the rest of my life.

The flight was a long one. There is a Naval Air Station on Adak and we made a scheduled stop there. The landing brought about more work on my prayer life. As we were descending I could see the Pacific out both sides of the aircraft. The ocean was still all I could see as we touched down! It was unnerving to say the least.

When we finally reached The Rock, Ricky and I were once again assigned to different shifts. The fire fighter's barracks was the third floor of the Civil Engineering Squadron dormitory. We were hoping to be roommates but it didn't happen for a couple of months. We fell to the tasks of our new jobs, making new friends, and learning our way around the island, which was pretty small and nothing but tundra covered hills and brown-to-black rocky beaches.

I remembered what my pastor at Northwest Baptist Church had told me before I left for basic training, "Don't trust those chaplains, even the Baptist ones. They are all liberals." Holding a private worship service in my room with a drunken roommate is a difficult and lonely task. Ricky went to the service at the chapel, which was right next door, and loved it. He encouraged me to go but I was stubborn. Then I received a visit from the choir director who was a non-commissioned officer in one of the shops for his real job. He told me he understood my concerns and reminded me it was going to be a long year if I tried to Lone Ranger it. He invited me to choir rehearsal and introduced me to Chaplain Wally Hucabee.

Wally was a Southern Baptist chaplain who taught me many things about the Air Force, Chaplaincy, and life. When the choir director PCS'd (permanent change of station/went on to another assignment) I was offered the job of chapel music coordinator. Sunday was my Kelly day (the special day for firefighters every two weeks you did not work with your shift) which worked out well and I was paid $10 per hour. Wally returned to the states after a few months and his replacement was another Southern Baptist Chaplain, Milton Tyler.

Milton was a wonderful fellow from Texas who loved disciple making. He immediately launched a group of us on a study of the Campus Crusade for Christ material, Ten Basic Steps Toward Christian Maturity. When we completed this he fed us the Billy Hanks Jr. discipleship course and we ate it up like desert.

There were lonely times but Kathy kept me going with letters, care packages, pictures of Amy, and phone calls. Kathy discovered if she called me on Sundays we could talk for 35 cents per minute, which was great considering we were six thousand miles apart. Words cannot describe how I looked forward to those calls.

I also looked forward to those packages filled with good stuff from home. The Reever would bring the mail out twice a week. The whole base held its breath on those days and when the high winds or fog cancelled the flight the bars would be full.

My 24-hour work shift would be busy with training, vehicle, equipment maintenance, aircraft standby duty, and once in a while an emergency run. In the evenings I would read and lift weights.

After roll call and the bus ride back to the main compound my day off would begin with breakfast at the chow hall. I would then go back to my room for a little Bible study and prayer before I went to the base gym. The gym was small but adequate. I played a lot of basketball and learned the game of racquetball. Several people would brave the cold wind and run outdoors when we were not under wind chill restrictions. I always ran laps in the gym. Before I left the island I was up to running five miles, 102 laps.

After lunch I would go to the chapel and work on my music. I had lots of great times hanging around the chapel for hours practicing music for the Protestant and Catholic services. I also read quite a lot that year. The base library was very small but how many books can you read in a year?

I requested and was granted leave to cover the time our baby was due. The C-section delivery was scheduled for May 22. The Reever cost $750 one way so commercial travel off the island was out of the question. The best option was to catch a hop on one of the military resupply flights out from Anchorage. If all else failed you could catch the Strategic Air Command Turn. There was a SAC detachment which flew a couple of RC135's on snoop missions against the Russians. Their headquarters was at Eielson AFB near Fairbanks, Alaska, and they rotated their people every Wednesday. They always made the trip even if it turned out to be impossible to land safely.

Kathy told me she had made flight reservations from Anchorage, through Seattle, Denver, and Kansas City to home beginning on Wednesday evening. My military leave papers were flexible and didn't start until you left the island. The Tuesday I was supposed to begin leave there were two flights scheduled to arrive from the mainland. The C130 and C141 flights were both scrubbed due to weather. I can't remember if it was wind or fog problems—the only kind of weather we had in the spring.

I was disappointed but knew the SAC Turn would make an attempt on Wednesday. Our Bible study was Tuesday night and during prayer time my friends really lifted me up and I felt peace about the trip. I went to bed feeling pretty good.

I awakened at midnight to someone pounding on the door, "Wake up West, you got a phone call in the dayroom!" I stumbled down the hall a little confused. Kathy was the only person who ever called me there. When I answered the phone I heard the Texas drawl of Ricky Pope who was on duty in the alarm center, "Hey Roomdog (military for roommate), scrape your whiskers and drag your bag. There's a Navy P3 on 12 mile final. They are stopping for fuel and can take on four hops. You're on the list and the chief is on his way to pick you up."

I ran to the room, shaved, and quickly dressed in my blues. There was a regulation which required active duty members on space available hops to travel in a class A uniform. The chief delivered me to Base Ops (Operations) with a few minutes to spare. I bought my four-dollar ticket and paid for a box lunch.

The Navy P3 Orion was on the final leg of a 30 day TDY (temporary duty assignment) flying their sub-chasing missions out of Adak. They had spent the last week in Japan on a boondoggle and were returning home. If they made their fuel stop at a base which had a customs officer they would be required to wait for them to come out in the middle of the night to inspect their coffee grounds and such. We did not have a customs agent so they chose to refuel on Shemya in the middle of the night.

The P3 crew of 20 was not very friendly to their Air Force brothers. The aircraft was full of Japanese silk pillows and things. My ditching seat for takeoff and landing was a seat belt attached to the deck near the rear door. I could lean my right shoulder against a small bulkhead. Sitting on the floor in my class A blues was not my idea of comfort but I couldn't beat the price and I was on my way home to Kathy and Amy and a brand new baby. I thanked God for answered prayer.

The flight to Mountain View Naval Air Station near San Jose, California, lasted eight hours and forty-five minutes. Having nowhere to sit but the floor and feeling the vibration of four noisy turbo prop engines made it the longest flight of my life. No one told us where to go when we arrived and deplaned. We four airmen walked across the wide ramp and finally got someone to point us toward the public bus stop. The bus ride to the San Jose Airport was quiet. No one spoke to us and we were tired. The other three Air Force guys were smart and changed into civilian clothes as soon as we arrived at the airport. I was in a hurry to arrange for connecting flights and I had always felt proud in my uniform so I did not.

I went from airline counter to airline counter asking for help with connections and no one could find a flight for me. I even asked for a flight to Seattle so I could connect with the flights Kathy had arranged for me. Someone finally told me they could sell me a ticket but my flight out of there was a standby booking with no guarantee.

The other guys seemed to have no trouble arranging flights home. I was very tired and starting to feel depressed and angry. It seemed like staying in uniform had been a bad idea. The women were especially hateful with their stares and non-friendly comments. I sat down and prayed.

When I refocused on the row of counters I noticed one counter had no customers, American Airlines I think it was. It was the only one I had not tried. I stepped up to the counter and explained my situation to a sharply dressed young man. He smiled and looked at his computer terminal for a couple of minutes. He looked up, smiled again and said, "If you can hang out here until 9:45 tonight, we'll fly you across the bay to San Francisco. After an hour there we will fly you to St. Louis and have you in Springfield by 8:30 tomorrow morning. How does that sound?"

It sounded heaven sent to me. I arrived home a day ahead of Kathy's arrangements and for a much smaller price tag. I learned a great deal on this trip. It would be years before I would willingly travel on commercial air in uniform again. The best lesson was God can put together an amazing plan, if you let Him.

I presented Kathy with a new pair of rings I had purchased for her and she presented me with a very pretty baby girl. We named her Elizabeth Janelle. She was a sweet and gentle baby and her sister Amy

Michelle liked her fine except at feeding times. She did not like the way her mother did it.

The month passed all too quickly. Only Kathy had come with me to the airport when I left the first time. She said Amy had tried to find me for days. We decided it would be best to include the girls this time. It had been hard the first time. It was unbearable the second. After hugs and kisses to Kathy, Amy, and Beth I leaned toward my military bearing, stood up tall, and walked away. Sunglasses could not hide the tracks of tears down my face. It was the hardest thing I had ever done. Kathy said it did help Amy and her.

My trip back to The Rock led me all the way to Fairbanks and Eielson AFB so I could catch the SAC Turn. Fairbanks in June was simply beautiful. Everything was green and growing right before your eyes. The shades had to be pulled at night so you could sleep. We made the flight out to Shemya without incident until we arrived. The island was socked in with heavy fog. Our flight crew was determined to land and support their people. They made three passes at the island to prove it. The pilot said he saw a window in the clouds open just after he started powering out of the last approach. That made for another sunny night in Fairbanks.

The pilot declared an in-flight emergency soon after we took off the next morning. I heard someone say something about a landing gear indicator but never really heard why. We made a lazy turn around Mt. McKinley and headed back for the base. It was very strange to look out on the edge of the runway and see firefighting and rescue vehicles chasing along beside us. I had seen this from the fire fighter's view many times. This was a first for me—but not the last.

We landed safely and were parked next to our replacement aircraft. Crew, passengers, and maintenance personnel formed a human chain and we quickly transferred all baggage and material to another KC135. We took off without further incident and landed on Shemya under clear skies and normal winds, a mere 40 knots.

Getting back on schedule was easy. The days were much longer but nothing like Fairbanks. I was spending more and more time in the gym and chapel. Even though I was growing in my faith I still suffered occasional anxiety. Through this, we solved one of my family's mysterious health problems.

I had long been plagued by a strange numbing of my fingers, hands, mouth, and tongue. I had mentioned it to doctors but they usually just gave me a strange look. It would always go away but leave me with a terrible headache back of my eyes. An incident on Shemya helped me understand my problem.

Once a month we would host a base-wide dinner and movie at the chapel. We had three white sheets sown together for a screen and would rent 16mm films from somewhere back in the world. This particular month we were showing *Jesus Christ, Superstar* and serving spaghetti with sides, catered from the Airman's club. We were planning to feed during intermission. I was asked to help haul food from the club which was a block away.

I carried a large pan of spaghetti then went directly in and sat down in the pews to watch the movie. The picture was soon blurry and I was struggling to focus. I asked one of my friends if the movie was out of focus and they said no. I left the chapel and sat down in the foyer. The signs on the wall were unreadable so I headed to my barracks next door and went to bed. As before, numbness started in my right fingers and progressed up my arm to my cheeks and tongue. This had happened before, in school, but it seemed worse this time and I was scared some.

After redressing I went back to the chapel and sat down again in the vestibule. I wanted help but was confused and didn't know what to do. Chaplain Milton Tyler saw me sitting and asked if I was all right. I tried to answer, "I don't think so," but it came out all jumbled. He and one of my chapel friends guided me immediately to the infirmary across the compound.

There were no medical doctors assigned to Shemya but we did have two competent medics. I described my symptoms and the onset as best I could and the medic on duty gave me Tylenol or something and put me to bed for the night. When I awoke the next morning he was waiting for me. He said I might have had an anxiety attack.

The way my faith in God was growing I was doubtful of his diagnosis. I told him I didn't think anxiety was the case. He said,

"Anybody stationed out here has earned an anxiety attack or two." He went on to say he believed I had hyperventilated. I was a nationally certified Emergency Medical Technician and I told him I was not doing the classic shallow huffing my training had described. He was ready for me.

He said, "That's only one way it can manifest itself." He opened a huge medical book on his desk and read every symptom I had displayed. He walked me through my activities the previous evening and convinced me when I stepped in to see the movie after heavy exertion I had chosen shallow, quiet breathing over the deep slow breathing I needed. This created a surplus of oxygen in my blood which caused my body to send some clear messages something was wrong. He prescribed a paper bag to breathe into. It worked.

As I approached the end of my year on Shemya I knew God had used it to change me. I had lost a significant amount of weight by working out every day. I had arrived weighing 210 pounds and left weighing 173. But the changes went much deeper. I had read God's word every day and diligently worked on memorizing scripture. I had worked on my music skills every day I was off from the Fire Department. I had even taken up ceramics for stress management. Thanks to Milton Tyler, I had become a serious and intentional disciple of Jesus.

One day Milton and I were looking for a table in the chow hall when we were invited to sit with an older gentleman we knew from chapel services. He was a civilian contractor assigned to one of the many top-secret missions on The Rock. As we were settling in he said, "Milton I'm glad you're here. I need to say something to Wayne and need you to bear witness." This man sang in the Chapel Choir for me and we did Bible study together. Immediately my mind began to search for anything I might have said or done to offend him.

He set my mind at ease when he told me how pleased he was that I would restart my education to pursue the call to ministry when I left Shemya. I had announced this to the Chapel family. Milton had been spending a good amount of time encouraging me and preparing my mind for college again. My friend continued, "Wayne, you are going to serve in lots of different Baptist churches. People in those churches are going to love you but they are also going to hurt you." I sat there in silence and he went on, "I don't know why we do it but I promise you, it will happen." He turned to Milton and said, "Am I telling Wayne the truth?" Milton nodded and said, "I'm afraid you are."

It was hard to say good-bye to my friends on Shemya. I had seen God work in many of their lives, not just mine. Milton and Ricky, along with some of the other firefighters, saw me off to the world from Base Ops. It was definitely a lump-in-the-throat moment. I was glad I had come to Shemya. I was a little fearful of what might lay beyond but I told myself God was in control. I'm not sure how strongly I believed it.

It took a week to process out of the Air Force at Elmendorf AFB. I spent my last weekend with the pastor of Sunset Hills Baptist Church and his family. Someone I had met on Shemya had told them I could sing. I sang three or four of my songs in the Sunday morning service. After lunch the pastor delivered me to another pastor on the east side of Anchorage. I sang several songs for the Eagle River Baptist Church in their evening service then accompanied their youth group and leaders to a nearby medium security prison for puppet gospel sharing and more of my music. I was impressed by the fact these prisoners had better digs than I had lived in during the past year.

I was glad to be going home to Kathy and the girls. I had committed to going back to college and pursuing God's plan for my call to ministry, whatever it was. It had been an amazing year. I will always be grateful to God for sending me there. This was the only year since 1973 the Would-be Woodsman had not hunted deer but the experience was worth the sacrifice.

Chapter 9

1980: Back In the World Adjustments

Kathy and the girls met me at the Springfield Airport and drove me to the little house at 1663 E. Blaine she had purchased. I was glad to be home and immediately took on some fix it projects she had lined up for me. When I went to see my parents for the first time I could tell my mom was shocked at the sight of me. The pale northern sun had not done much for my complexion and I weighed 173 pounds. My mother asked me right away if I had cancer.

The Air Force had been good for me and I missed it. There is something very secure about the military. While it is true you might be sent anywhere in the world on a moment's notice, the paycheck is always there on time, medical care is always available for you and your family, and you get thirty days of vacation each year.

Southwest Baptist University had accepted me for the spring semester. It was exciting but was going to be expensive. It would take all of my monthly GI Bill money to pay tuition even though I received every small scholarship I was eligible for. The 60-mile daily commute would also take some money. I enrolled with a 17 hour load and waited for the semester to begin.

I drew unemployment benefits and worked on our little house while I waited for the semester to begin. The emotional strain of being reunited with Kathy was puzzling. Leaving the Air Force with no idea where the money necessary for expenses was going to come from took its toll on me.

One day after not being selected for a music and youth minister position at a local church I was particularly depressed and fearful. I was on the front porch trimming the bottom of the front door so it would clear our shag carpeting. Desperation gripped my heart as I worked. Where was the money going to come from? Was I really college material? Should I re-enlist? In my spirit I cried out to God.

The postman delivered the mail. I spoke briefly with him then looked at the mail in my hands. Among the bills was an envelope from Alaska—Eagle River Baptist Church. I opened the envelope and found a nice thank you note for singing at their church and the prison. Folded in the letter was a check for 35 dollars.

Stunned, I carried the mail inside and sat down in a chair. I was overwhelmed at this unexpected gift. That amount was not going far toward securing our finances but I felt it was an on-time word from the Lord that He would meet our needs. I felt weak and foolish for having fallen into doubt. I felt glad to be reminded that He is my source. I called Kathy at work and told her I felt everything would be all right.

Just before the semester started I landed a job with my old employer, Ozark Wholesale Grocer. My job as a night shipping clerk began at 6:00 and finished at midnight. It was a tough schedule.

I had a 07:30 a.m. music theory class five days a week. I would leave the house at 06:30 and deliver Amy and Beth to the babysitter. The drive to Bolivar would land me in class without a minute to spare. My classes finished at 15:00 (3 p.m.) and I would return to Springfield, pick up the girls and take them home. I would feed them a snack and play with them until Kathy got home. She worked as a bookkeeper under her father at Springfield Lincoln Mercury. We would usually meet at the door for a hello and goodbye kiss as I headed out.

After my shift at the warehouse I would stop by the local 7-11store to purchase $5.00 worth of gas to get me to school and back. Max had loaned us a pale green 1971 Chevrolet to use for the commute. I was grateful even though the trunk was usually flooded with musty rainwater.

It was a long and hard semester but I finished with a 3.75 GPA. I enrolled at Southwest Missouri State University for summer classes because it was much cheaper and, by then, I had been hired as Music and Youth Director for Northwest Baptist Church in Springfield. My plan was to return to SBU in the fall but while I attended SMSU I felt a sense of peace and release about the necessity to attend a Baptist school. As a married, veteran, commuting student I did not really fit in with SBU campus life and did not feel the need for the nurture of a Christian campus. I continued at SMSU as a full-time student in the fall.

Northwest Baptist Church is where I was baptized in 1972. The pastor then was John Doolittle. The original church building was destroyed by arson while Kathy and I were in Washington. They purchased the vacant church buildings on the corner of East Avenue and Turner streets under Pastor Troy Rhoden's leadership. The location was just a couple of blocks from my grandfather's house. Moving into this church complex was quite an upgrade from the old building.

It made life easier in many ways. My GI Bill money went further. We spent a lot less money on gas and I could work at the church between classes when necessary. Troy and I became good friends. I began to discover much about the ministry I had never even dreamed of— good and bad.

Troy's in-laws owned Springfield Asphalt Sealing Company. They would hire Troy and me for big jobs when they needed extra hands. Troy had worked with them for years before he entered the ministry and was very skilled at applying the material. I had a strong back and legs and hauled the material to him in five gallon buckets. The extra money was helpful but I sure earned it.

My pastor friend saved his extra income money so he could move his family to Ft. Worth and seminary. He accepted several jobs during the fall and took me along as his fetch-and-tote. One job involved painting the tennis courts at SMSU and since it was a government contract the prevailing wage was in play. I earned about $50 from the job and, with Kathy's blessing, purchased my first compound bow from OTASCO (Oklahoma Tire and Supply Company). It was made by Indian Archery and featured a plastic coated metal riser, a built-in three pin sight, and continuous coated cable which served as the bowstring. It was rated at fifty pounds of pull. I do not remember hunting with it in 1980 though I surely did.

I should probably mention the tough time I had readjusting to family life. The hectic rhythm of our lives added to the difficulty. Kathy and I had both changed during our year of separation. I had become more introspective and had been working on my cognitive abilities. Kathy once complained I had didn't even talk the same way.

Kathy had grown in confidence. She had been totally responsible for our children and home-front preparation for our future. Six thousand miles was a great distance in the days before the internet and cell phones. Her parents were great supporters but she learned to be strong. She bought a 1974 Mercury Marquis and had handled everything well as she purchased our house. She could do anything and I was proud of her.

The biggest difficulty in reunions of this nature is the problem of roll identity. I did not know where I fit in with my family and Kathy had become used to being everything. At times it did not even seem like it was my family. I felt unwanted, unneeded, and on the brink of depression. Kathy has never been one to talk much about emotional things. She just thought I was weird. She was at least partially right.

One day when I finished with school early I stopped by the house and pulled all of my clothes out of the hamper and washed them. I had taken care of my own things for a year. We had gotten along great over the phone and in letters but living together was a struggle. I'm not sure why I did my laundry.

I might have been reaching back to a simpler place and time but I think I was trying to send Kathy a message—I felt like I did not belong in her family group. She did not seem to notice my action or hear my cry. More than twenty years later she told me she had noticed and it had scared her to death.

There was not much time for Would-be Woodsman adventures that year but I did manage a one weekend hunt with my father-in-law. Just before I went in the service Max and Ardelle had bought a cabin on Bulls Shoals Lake near Protem, Missouri. The cabin and lots were the last on the road to the cove where their dock was located. There were acres and acres of Corp of Engineers land available to hunt.

When we arrived at the cabin the evening before opening day I ventured out in the dark and hung a stand in a tree on the edge of an opening in the cedars. I was unaware of my surroundings and it became evident the next morning.

I climbed into my stand well before daylight to discover my perch was less than 75 yards from another cabin. I could hear the occupants loudly preparing for their drunken hunt. It was very disconcerting when one of them stepped out onto the porch and fired his rifle into the air.

Just before daylight it started to rain. Determined to be tough I shivered in my home made stand. Around 9:30 I heard shooting to the north. About 15 minutes later I picked up motion I first thought was a dog. It turned out to be a forked horn buck. I watched it skirt the edge of the small field I guarded. Overconfident, I drew a bead on the buck and fired. I was using Max's Winchester 30-30 which had a hood over the front sight. I can only guess that I forgot to line up the front and rear sights because I missed very badly. It was the only deer we saw that year. I do remember one other thing from that soggy season: five 30-30 rounds were missing from my gear at the end of the hunt. I assumed I had lost them in the woods. There's that dangerous word again.

Chapter 10

1981: God's Word on Our Future

In August of 1981 I helped move Troy and his family to Southwestern Baptist Theological Seminary in Ft. Worth, Texas. I had begun talking with the pastor and personnel committee at Tatum Chapel Baptist Church about serving as their Minister of Music and Youth.

I loved the people of Northwest, and still do, but without Troy's leadership Kathy and I felt it was time to make a move. Tatum Chapel was a growing country/suburban church in western Greene County with strong programs in music and youth. Tommy Harper was the pastor. I learned to love him and his family.

Fall was really busy with the new church and school but I managed to find a little time to hunt. My Dad's first cousin and her husband owned a piece of the Old West Place out in the far eastern end of Greene County. Ray and Geraldine Maybe were gracious and invited me to hunt on their property. Ray was a World War II veteran and recognized my struggle to adjust to civilian life and helped me name my longing for the simple life of the military.

I saw several deer while scouting and caught glimpses of a couple while archery hunting on the Maybe's land. I also hunted on the Swadley place near Tatum Chapel with my bow and arrow. While hunting there one afternoon a small hawk tried to land on me while I was perched in one of their trees. I was learning total, head-to-toe, camouflage can lead to some close encounters with all kinds of critters. Other than some excitement, nothing came of my first real season of bow hunting in Missouri.

I took Ray and Gerry's grandson, Brian Wright, hunting on opening day of the gun deer season. He was a delightful young man, full of energy and desire for anything having to do with the outdoors. Brian had a special gift when it came to outdoor adventures. If you wanted to see game or catch fish, just tag along with Brian Wright.

While we hunted on his grandparents' place he came upon a small herd of antlerless deer and just started firing slugs in among them. We had a long talk about sportsmanship, ethics, and marksmanship. Other than being a bit of an outlaw, he was fun to have around. I was not too far removed from outlaw days myself.

I also hunted again with Max near his cabin on Bull Shoals Lake. Exploring many acres of Corps of Engineer lands was enlightening but disappointing. The only wildlife I encountered were squirrels—not even a drunken hunter this time.

One other incident is worth mentioning. The last time I hunted with Max's Winchester had been the year before. Evidently Max had not touched his gun since then either. The Friday evening we arrived at the cabin I took the rifle out of the case and worked the action. To my great surprise a shell ejected. There were four other rounds in the magazine. I was embarrassed but glad no one had been hurt—mystery solved and no harm done—lesson learned.

The really big event of that fall had to do with Kathy. She had been in a great mood, enjoying our new church and making new friends. Around the first of December things changed. She seemed angry but refused to admit it. She insisted nothing was wrong and would not talk to me about it. I kept at her until she was finally angry enough at me to speak. She said, "I'm either really bad sick or pregnant, and I don't know which I would rather be!" I backed off and suggested she go to see her doctor. She refused.

After my first class the next morning, I called the office of the doctor who had delivered Elizabeth and was able to get an appointment for later in the morning. I called Kathy at her work and told her I would pick her up at 11:00. She didn't even argue.

I skipped my second class and waited at home. Deeply concerned about Kathy's health and our future, I prayed. I certainly did not want Kathy to be sick but I knew we were having a tough time financially with two children. How would we make it with another? I poured my heart out to God and asked him for some help, some encouragement from His word. I picked up the Thompson Chain Reference King James Bible Kathy had sent me on Shemya and prayerfully let it flop open.

This is certainly not the most mature approach to Bible study but I wasn't concerned about scholarly credibility. I was concerned about Kathy and our family and I was desperate for a Word from God. My Bible fell open to 2 Chronicles, Chapter 20. I read where King Jehoshaphat led his troops out to face the enemies of Judah. God had told him through a prophet if he would be faithful, He would deliver them. As an act of faith, the king sent his best praising singers and musicians out to lead the troops to the battle. They praised God all the way singing, "Give thanks to the Lord, for his love endures forever." When they reached their enemies, they discovered the three armies awaiting them had annihilated each other.

I felt God was speaking to me. I said to Him, "Lord, do you mean you want me to praise you now, before I know the answer from the doctor? I want to praise You but I just need a little room to get my thinking turned around." After praising God out loud in prayer for a while, I asked Him to give me a new song to praise Him with. My piano was three feet away so I moved there and began singing and playing a song I had never heard before. I entitled it, "I Praise the Lord."

Around noon we found out our third child was well on the way. I was excited and pleased and assured Kathy everything was going to be fine—I had God's Word on it.

Chapter 11

1982: Busyness and Growth

Sometime in 1982 we moved from 1663 E. Blaine to a huge apartment under Barnes Town and Country Store out west of Springfield on old Route 66. The highway was then called U.S. 266 but historical markers and abandoned gas stations pointed to its past glory.

The store was owned by the family of one of my choir members at TCBC. The apartment was amazing. It had been the residence of the original store owners and was the nicest place I had ever lived in. The huge living room with fireplace worked well with the three bedrooms, two-and-a-half bathrooms, kitchen, dining room, laundry room, covered patio, and extensive porches. It was a very nice place to live and it placed us on the field near the people of the church we served and loved.

Early in the year I started planning a youth mission trip to Basalt, Colorado. I had never attempted such an extensive project. Kathy was a great help and coached me through the detailed planning necessary. The summer promised to be a busy one so I did not take a full summer school schedule.

Every year since our return to Springfield we had taken a couple of weeks to work at the Greene County Baptist Association camps at Baptist Hill near Mount Vernon, Missouri. This year I served as head lifeguard and Kathy led the pre-camper program of the girl's camp. Amy Michelle was four, Elizabeth Janelle was three, and Kathy was very pregnant with the baby I thought would be named Kristen Lavelle.

The weather was hot and the cabin was not air conditioned so I rigged a portable air conditioner in a window to help Kathy and the girls sleep better. Kathy was miserable but did her job wonderfully well and with a smile. I worked the first three days of the boy's camp week and returned home Thursday morning.

Our children were scheduled to be born after Amy's C-section delivery. On Friday, July 2, 1982 I drove Kathy to Cox hospital in Springfield where she was prepped for the surgery.

Earlier in the pregnancy Kathy's doctor had performed an ultrasound exam and offered to tell us the baby's gender. It was a very new thing in those days and Kathy did not want to know so I went along with her decision, of course.

Like most dads I hoped for a son when Amy was born. She was such a delight to me and Elizabeth was such a sweet girl I had decided it was great to be a father to girls. I assumed (a hard lesson to unlearn) God had chosen me to raise girls. We had previously held the name David Wayne in reserve in case any of our babies were boys. This time we had not even discussed a boy name. Our baby's name would be Kristen Lavelle West.

I kissed Kathy and headed out to the fathers waiting room. This hospital still did not allow anyone in the surgery suite for C-section deliveries. Thank heaven! I thought surely it would be a little while so I called the church office to take care of some business. There were several other men in the room. My back was to the inner doorway as I heard a female voice say, "You have a fine baby boy." I knew she could not be talking to me so I continued with my phone conversation until I heard the voice again saying, "Are you Mr. West?" In shock, I acknowledged my identity. She was holding a baby in a bundle and she was right—He was a fine baby boy.

When I got to see Kathy we discussed our delight and surprise. The name David Wayne had gone a little stale for me so I suggested William Wayne West Junior. Kathy stated he was too little to be called William, Wayne would be too confusing, and Junior was out of the question. She said, "If I can call him Billy, he can have your name." It really pleased me because I had always liked my name even though I did not always like myself.

A week later I left for Basalt, Colorado, with 30 youth and nine adults. Our mission involved leading a Vacation Bible School for a struggling church in Basalt. Basalt is between Glenwood Springs and Aspen. There was lots of construction going on in the Aspen area and most construction workers and their families lived in mobile home parks around Basalt.

The church was in a split-entry home. The upper floor was open and served as the auditorium. The rest of the house was used for education, nursery and an office. We stayed in another church about ten miles away. Someone had donated the land and funds for the building but it was not visible and accessible to people. Roaring River Baptist church was about to die but it was a great place to house and feed a mission team.

In addition to leading the VBS our Youth Choir did concerts in two churches and we used our puppet ministry to reach and invite children in the mobile home parks to VBS. We managed an afternoon in the hot spring pool in Glenwood Springs. The most amazing and difficult thing about the trip is we all traveled in a school bus.

There was a great mechanic in our church who had rebuilt the bus engine and installed a window air conditioner powered by a gas generator mounted on the rear bumper. We had removed about half of the seats and padded the floor with six inches of foam rubber and covered it with carpet. This allowed for sleeping because we drove straight out and straight back, over two thousand miles. Taking the seats out was probably not safe and by the time we got home, the kids were fighting over who would get to sit in an old school bus seat. Thank God He made the trip with us.

It was a wonderful event and I learned quite a lot about ministry and leadership. The adults on the team were outstanding people and their work was superb. They allowed me to focus on my leadership and spiritual care responsibilities.

I was a music major at the university, a minister of music and youth in a Baptist church, a husband, and a father. My responsibilities did not leave much room for the Would-be Woodsman in me and hunting was pretty much a bust in 1982. I bow hunted on neighbors around the church and even launched some arrows to no avail.

Bow hunting was and is a learn-as-you-go thing for me. I invited my pastor, Tommy Harper and his oldest son, Larry, to go with me to Max's cabin on Bull Shoals Lake for a two day bow hunt. On the drive down to Protem we listened to the radio as the St. Louis Cardinals won the World Series.

I don't think Tommy had ever bow hunted deer before but he was game to try. I never had until the first time myself. We did not see any deer and I'm sure my guests were disappointed.

One other memory hangs with me from the trip. I had ventured out on a long wooded point. The last couple of hundred yards of the peninsula was actually in Arkansas. I hunkered down not far from the state line to listen and watch. The sky became overcast toward the end of the day and as the light was fading fast I realized I did not have a flashlight with me.

I gave up my fruitless task and headed back toward the cabin, hustling to get back before dark. About halfway up the point I became confused on the trail. I stopped and found myself standing in a saddle. The trail rose slightly to my front and was guarded by large oaks and pines with some kind of vine spreading across and up from left to right. I had seen that view before on the way in.

I turned back to look the way I thought I had come and was surprised to find myself standing in a saddle. The trail, rising slightly to my front, was guarded by large oaks and pines with some kind of vine spreading across and up from left to right. I turned again, and then again. Soon I was not sure which way I should be going. Without the sun or a compass, I became totally disoriented and experienced some panic.

I finally chose a direction and started walking. After about a hundred yards I sensed the trail descending. I executed an about face and found my way home in the dark. It has always been difficult to make decisions when the choices are similar but this experience was bizarre and memorable. It convinced me to always carry a compass and a light. It also reminded me God's Word is my compass and light—I should never go anywhere without it.

Fall firearms deer hunting was even less memorable. I remember hunting around the cabin with Max and making an evening trip to Dora to see how the hunters there were doing. The only deer we saw were alongside the road at night but 1982 was still a great and blessed year in my life. Among other blessings, I had a son who shared my name.

Chapter 12

1983: Maynard Hill Lessons

Not long after the first of the year my pastor, Tommy, spoke to me several times about my need to move on to seminary after graduation, expected in May. He made a good case. What he said made sense but I was really enjoying my work with the choir and young people at Tatum Chapel Baptist Church. I corresponded with the registrar at Midwestern Baptist Theological Seminary in Kansas City, Missouri. It was the closest Southern Baptist Seminary. The Baptist Student Union director at SMSU and an older youth pastor at a large church in town were alumni and recommended the school.

Kathy and I discussed and prayed about whether we should go to seminary immediately or later but didn't feel ready to go. I wanted to work at TCBC until my first class of junior high students graduated from high school. My student and music programs were growing and getting stronger, I thought.

During a Wednesday night church business meeting Tommy announced I would be leaving the church after graduation to attend seminary. I finally got the message; he was ready for me to go. It hurt me and broke my heart. I did not understand and made a huge mistake.

I did not believe that Tommy could possibly be right and God was ready for us to move on. I whined and complained to some church leaders because I felt Tommy had treated me unfairly. I had prayed regularly for God's will to be reality in my life but was unwilling to hear anything that wasn't in my plan. I should have done my crying to God and sought His will. Instead I had a pity party and defended myself to others.

Kathy and I made a trip to Kansas City to check out the seminary after which I applied to the Master of Religious Education degree program and was accepted. About then I was completing the difficult and culminating acts required of every music education major. I served as a student teacher at Willard Junior High School for the first eight weeks of the spring semester. This is where a great number of my younger youth attended school. It made the experience enjoyable for me.

I also worked on my senior recital which I performed in the second half of the semester. We scheduled the concert on a Saturday afternoon so family and friends could attend. My vocal coach, Dale Everrett, also performed as my accompanist. He was an amazing musician. I sang four sets of three songs each in four different languages: German, Italian, French, and English. I mangled one of the French pieces but no one seemed to notice except Dale who he said he was impressed at my recovery. So was I, but mostly I was elated to successfully complete this enormous and daunting project.

To my knowledge, I was the first West of our branch of this clan to graduate from college. I was proud and glad to be done with it but by the evening of graduation day I felt myself slipping into a depression similar to the one I experienced when I left the Air Force. What was next in our lives? I did not feel confident about going to seminary and didn't know why so I fell back to a comfortable zone and visited with an Air Force recruiter about becoming an officer.

He described to me a program where the Air Force was taking in some college graduates too old to be trained as aircrew. I was interested and began making preparations to go to Kansas City to take a battery of tests. Preparing for these tests was like getting ready to take the Graduate Record Exam. This study reminded me I was weak in mathematics. The weakness was not because I was incapable of or afraid of math. I just had never taken any more than I had to.

As I was cleaning out my office at the church one afternoon I received word from the recruiter I had passed all sections of the exam except math. He quickly told me he was pretty sure he could get a waiver for me. My life had taught me some things about seeking God's will. One of which is: If you have to press too hard on a door of opportunity, God may me be protecting you from what is on the other side. I thanked the recruiter for his efforts but called off the quest for a commission.

I was out of a job with no prospects and no clear word from God about going to seminary. Even if I did go to seminary, there were still several months with a family to feed and a personal need to work. I talked with Kathy about trying to pick up some grub work with Springfield Asphalt Sealing Company before I paid them a visit. Don Anstine remembered my work with his son-in-law Troy. He hired me on the spot and made me a crew leader. The steep learning curve nearly overwhelmed me but I relished the leadership opportunity and the hot, hard, and exacting work.

The work was pre-sunrise to post-sunset seven days a week if it was not raining. After a while they gave me every other Sunday off so I could attend Second Baptist Church with Kathy and the kids. It was the toughest, nastiest work I have ever done but I discovered I could take pride in even such a filthy job if I did it ". . . as unto the Lord." (Colossians 3:23)

We moved back into Springfield in July. We crowded into a small three bedroom house on Page Street. It was close to Springfield Lincoln Mercury where Kathy worked and not far from Second Baptist Church or Kathy's folks. The next door neighbor was a man I had worked with at Ozark Grocer. His daughters watched the kids for us from time to time.

One unsettling event from that summer has stayed with me. When I would finish a day of applying asphalt sealer I would be very, very dirty. The coal tar and chemical smell of my clothes would make other people's eyes water. There was no shower at the SASCO building so I kept a blanket over the front seat of my 1974 Mercury Comet. I had to stop for gas one evening and after pumping went into the convenience store to write a check. I certainly did not look or smell like a college graduate and as I placed my buffed up signature on the check the middle-aged female store clerk said, "Don't you think that's a little much for you?" What could I say?

After a long summer of hard work I was not ready to leave for seminary. Not because I was making a great deal of money, I wasn't. I was still unclear about my motives for going to seminary. To uproot my family and move to a strange place when I was unsure of the direction of my future ministry did not seem fair to them or sensible to me.

Asphalt sealing work slowed down and I began to long for the wood shaded lanes of the Ozarks. The summer had been hot and nasty but I was encouraged by the well-known fact that after every summer comes the fall, and with the fall, cooler breezes and dreams of deer hunting coming true.

I was invited on an early October bow hunt with my Sunday School teacher, Ed. We went with a couple of men from Second Baptist Church, including my pastor, Dr. James Reimer. Ed had seen my 13 point deer mount. As we traveled together in the predawn darkness he mentioned it to Dr. Reimer who asked me from the front seat, "Have you ever considered selling it?" I laughed a little and said, "Who would buy it?" I could tell immediately I had offended him as he said, "Well, some people collect them, you know. Whitetail racks are all uniquely beautiful, God's artwork." I didn't know that and trying to recover replied, "Wow, I didn't realize that."

The hunt was enjoyable but relatively uneventful. I was touched and impressed when Ed gathered us around the back end of his blazer and led us in a prayer for the hunt before we separated to find our way to stand locations in the dark. He prayed a prayer of gratitude for creation and our dominion over the animals. He prayed for safe and ethical hunting and once again thanked God for the privilege of being off work and in His woods.

The next Sunday Jim Reimer asked me to bring my deer mount by his office some time. The next rainy day I did. He seemed impressed and said, "I do not have a good southern Missouri whitetail in my collection. That's a fine rack" I asked him, "What do you think it is worth?" After a slight pause and another look at the mount he said, "Four or five hundred dollars." He could see the shock on my face and quickly added, "I wouldn't want to give that much cash for it but I would be willing to do some trading." I stammered something and he continued, "You need a deer rifle don't you?" I wondered how he knew I always borrowed guns from my father-in-law. I must have said something on our bow hunt. He continued, "I have a brand new Remington 742, 30-06 still in the box. I could put a scope on it for you and throw in some cash to boot. We'll work out the details later."

I didn't even know what a 742 was until he described it. I told him I would have to think about it. It was very tempting. My father-in-law was always gracious about sharing his firearms but I hated to have to depend on him so much. I spoke with one of the owners at work who was a big hunter and photographer. He assured me of the value of the Remington 742 and pointed out that while seeing the mount every day was a good reminder of past hunts, I couldn't carry it in the woods for future adventures. He offered to take a picture of my mount so I would not lose it completely. The picture was taken and I traded my trophy.

A week or so later I received a radio call in my work truck. Dr. Reimer wanted me to stop by the church. We were working on that side of town so it was easy to do. He told me our music director had cancelled going to Enid, Oklahoma, to do a revival with him. He also said he could pay me $100 for the rest of the trophy deal or I could go with him to Oklahoma and lead music for him. He assured me I would make more than a hundred dollars. Work was definitely slowing down so I agreed. There was a downside—it was during the one week of gun deer season and I would only be able to hunt the first Saturday and the second weekend.

A few days later I managed an evening out at the Maybe acreage. I had placed a borrowed hang-on stand on the back side of a hilltop pasture. After a couple of hours watching I noticed movement up the drain from my position. At first and once again I thought it was a dog but as it drew closer I could see it was a forked horn buck. I was very aware this was the best opportunity so far in my bow hunting escapades and my heart rate showed it.

The little buck moved beneath me and out into a tractor trail which came down off the field. It was perfect. I drew my bow, selected a spot, and released my arrow with the deer less than ten yards away. The arrow stuck in the ground beneath the deer, which jumped, snorted, and made haste to disappear. I was stunned and disappointed. How could I have missed?

Dejected, my eyes fell to the bow in my lap. The riser of the bow was coated with vinyl plastic. The plastic on the front edge of the shelf was scuffed with a reddish color. My arrow vanes were red. It was pretty obvious I had forgotten to place the arrow back up on the rest before I fired. A tough lesson—many things can go wrong when archery hunting. A little buck fever can derail the best laid setup.

I was invited to return to Suzie and Bill's farm in Ozark County for the gun deer season. My excitement was barely containable as I prepared to hunt opening day before heading out to Oklahoma with Jim Reimer.

After I arrived—down home—I was delighted to learn I would be given the opportunity to hunt the Maynard Hill again. One of the second cousins (younger brother to the would-be cotton tailed rabbit spotlighter) would be hunting off of the pond bank near the gate. Not long after daylight I heard him shoot. It took about ten minutes for him to travel to my default pine tree location. He didn't have a knife to field dress the small deer he had shot. I don't remember whether it was a buck or a doe but I do remember being a little angry he had fouled my set up for the morning hunt.

I loaned him my sharp knife and off he went. My anger was slight and didn't last long because I remembered years before, I had done the same thing to Homer the Deerslayer. He had been hunting very near the place where this deer had been killed. After the interruption I could not seem to concentrate so I climbed down and went to see Charlie's deer. While I was admiring his deer and reclaiming my knife he indicated he would continue to hunt in the same location.

Still hunting (moving slowly hoping to see deer before they see you) was a skill I needed to work on so I told him my plan to walk around his aunt's pasture and hunt down the drain from the west. There was a good chance I would push another deer by him so he was more than willing for me to make the attempt.

It was difficult to make myself move slowly and keep my eyes peeled for anything that might be a part of a deer but I made myself do it. I successfully crossed the field and started moving along the brushy drain which headed at the paved roadway. After covering 30 or so yards I was excited to see a deer opposite me, working down the deepening hollow. At first I thought he had seen me but he was just moving along, unpressured put quick. The wind was in my favor.

I dropped to one knee and studied the situation. He was unaware of my presence and it looked like he would step into an opening in the trees and brush about 50 yards away, maybe less. I could see it was definitely a buck. Slowly, I raised the rifle and tried to find the deer in my scope. I couldn't see it. Panic started to rise in my throat. I remembered reading something about a trick for such a situation. Focusing on the deer I brought the scope to my shooting eye with both eyes open. All I could see was brown. It finally dawned on me the deer was filling my scope view.

Earlier, in my pine tree perch, I had dialed the variable scope up to nine and had forgotten to set it back to low magnification. Bad things can happen when you are unfamiliar with your equipment and use your scope in place of binoculars. It should have been simple to readjust the scope but having a buck in front of me addled my common sense. As I followed the deer through the scope I began to discern his anatomy and found his right shoulder. Finally, he presented a clear shot, I thought. I fired and he staggered before running on down the drain which had developed into more of a ravine. He was making a lot of noise, crashing and thrashing his way along.

You would think by that time in my journey as the Would-be Woodsman I would understand deer don't usually just lie down where you shoot them. Nonetheless, I was very troubled he did not so respond to my 30-06. I moved directly to where the deer had been standing and began to search for sign. I expected to see blood and plenty of it. Anxiety increased as I found none. It was obvious I was looking in the right place because ground was scuffed where he staggered before taking off.

As I looked around something I didn't expect to see caught my eye back up the slope toward my original position. White, ragged fibers were visible on the lower side of a one-and-a-half inch oak limb hanging down from a tree. It didn't take me long to figure out I had shot the limb slightly right of center before it struck the deer. I immediately realized things were not good. The bullet would have expended much it its energy on the tree and had surely mushroomed and changed shape drastically before it struck the deer—probably farther forward than I had aimed. The high power setting of the scope had focused past the limb and on the deer. Not good. Not good at all.

Scattered splotches of blood guided me to the bottom of the draw where it was joined by several other drains to form the large hollow between the Maynard Hill and the Billy Mack place. This was where the deer had been found on the infamous morning back in 1975 when I let everyone know I was some kind of marksman. The bungled shot I had just made was triggering an emotional flashback to that day and added to my panic.

I caught a glimpse of the deer moving into the thick draw which ran up to the north end of the Maynard Hill just as I found a sapling marked with blood and several small bone fragments. I knew I was near Charlie and a whistle got a quick answer. I moved to his location and hatched my plan. I said, "Give me fifteen minutes to climb to the Maynard Hill field and get in position." I specified, "Then work slowly up the steep drain and push the deer out to me." It seemed simple enough.

I hustled uphill past the pond and into position. Even though I was in pretty good shape I sat down to rest a minute. There should have been eight to ten minutes before Charlie started his mini-drive. I should have guessed he did not own a watch. No sooner had my backside met the ground than the wounded buck burst out of the drain, saw me, and broke to his left and into the woods along the field. His hoofs striking the ground were unusually loud. He was definitely hurt—definitely my deer.

I rose to my knees and tried to find the deer in my scope, desperate to finish the job I had begun with the first hunting shot fired out of the rifle I was so proud of. As I panned and scanned through the scope for the buck I received a horrifying shock. It happened so fast.

I sensed movement and saw dark brown. As I was straining to identify the animal so I could make a better, killing shot the thing turned and there was Charlie's face, with my crosshairs on his nose. He wore no hunter orange over his brown insulated coveralls. His hair was shoulder length and also brown. It was a good thing I had not eaten breakfast before the hunt because I surely would have tossed it. You know I climbed on him about the timing but I really chewed him out about the lack of hunter orange.

We hauled Charlie's deer back to the farm and met everyone else over breakfast. The general consensus was to get Homer the Deerslayer's dogs after my wounded deer but I stubbornly held them off. I was trying hard not to break my promise to God. Hunting with dogs was illegal but very tempting. I skipped the morning drives and went back to the Maynard Hill to continue my search. It was my first duty in this disturbing situation. Losing a deer due to a poor shot was a big thing. This was the first such occurrence for the Would-be Woodsman. It bothered me even more because it was a buck. I didn't like it one bit.

I searched for what seemed like hours up and down the brushy and wooded slope north of the Maynard Hill. No sign of the deer's passage was evident to me even in the places where I knew he had been. Looking back I realize I was suffering from the swirling-mind, self-scolding, and emotional panic I often suffer when I mess up anything.

Finally, I sat down to rest and think. I was not very far from the pond where Charlie had been hunting. The Would-be Woodsman was sick with disappointment. I took inventory of my related sins for the day, so far. I had made a huge mistake with the unfamiliar optics. Time and money had limited practice with my new firearm. I had asked a young man to enter into a quickly hatched plan which had nearly cost him his life. Even though he was partially at fault for not wearing orange, I should have recognized the danger. I was moving too fast in my search for sign and tracking the wounded buck—too upset. The only thing I had done right so far was not give in to the pressure to hunt my deer with dogs. The temptation was still there and growing by the minute.

I thought the buck was probably a nice one with a good rack though I really couldn't say for sure. Every deer is a trophy for the Would-be Woodsman. Losing one to poor woodsmanship would be unthinkable. I did not want to give up but I did not know what to do next.

Prayer was something I engaged in on a regular basis but I had never prayed about a hunting situation. It has always seemed silly to me to consider praying about the outcome of a sporting event like football or baseball. I had so far applied the same rule to hunting but I was desperate now. As a general rule, when I have a problem, I talk to the Lord about it. What could it hurt?

Closing my eyes to shut out the distractions of the beautiful woods that hid my deer, I prayed something like this: "Lord, I feel kind of silly talking to you about this deer but I am in over my head. I know I messed up with the shot and I hate it that the deer is suffering because of me. I do not want to lose this deer. I know I don't deserve it, but would you please help me find this buck? Thanks for keeping me from shooting Charlie. Amen."

I rested a while longer and ate an apple. Looking up the slope I realized I was sitting on an old tractor trail. It angled downhill to the northeast and was well defined by the parallel depressions in the forest floor. I got up and started moving down the trail and had scarcely gone

20 yards when I received the shock of my Would-be Woodsman life. There was my buck, standing in the middle of the trail.

We stared at each other and everything seemed to go into slow motion but my motion was slower than his. I did not even get my gun up before he ran out of range then out of sight. The rest of the day went by in kind of a daze. I caught glimpses of the deer from time to time but never had a shot I thought I could make.

The trip back to Springfield was a long one as I pondered the day. Losing the buck was a big thing but there was an even bigger problem eating at my heart. I had asked the Lord to help me, but didn't really expect him to. I was paralyzed to inaction when He did. Was my faith in Him regarding other things so weak?

Jim Reimer and I left for Enid, Oklahoma, immediately after church the next day. We led revival services at Liberty Baptist Church Sunday night through Friday night. Jim had been pastor at another Enid church and enjoyed the reunion with old friends. I had a lot of time on my hands, most of which I spent reliving the past Saturday morning.

One notable experience was an afternoon of hunting with one of Jim's friends. Danny Weldon was a one-of-a-kind man. His name should have been Daniel Boone. He was an exceptional outdoorsman and very successful hunter—born out of time it seemed. The week we were there was the week between deer seasons in Oklahoma. Danny took us out to call coyotes. I was just along for the experience. Jim killed a brute of a dog when Danny called in a whole pack.

I tried to concentrate on my musical responsibilities for the revival but I admit I was really glad to finish and head home on Friday night with $300 in my pocket. It was about 2:00 A.M. when I arrived home. I gathered my gear and headed back to Ozark County. I had a job to finish.

Arriving down home at 4:30, I did not want to awaken anyone at the house so I just pulled my car off the road along the lane to the Maynard Hill. Kathy's cousin, Clyde, woke me up by beating on the car roof just as the sky was beginning to lighten. As I stepped out of the car he commenced to dog me about my fancy gun and poor marksmanship. What could I say? He told me some coon hunters had bayed my wounded deer Thursday night. It was sick and the meat was lost so they shot it and left it in the woods.

I was sick too. The morning passed with me sitting in the woods with a rifle. I wouldn't call it hunting. As I hashed over the events of my deer season I decided mine was over. I had taken a buck, even though there would be no venison eaten by anyone but coyotes. I had taken my shot and harvested the buck. I decided I would not check the deer because I knew it would be too decomposed to move. In my mind, my gun tag was filled and to continue hunting did not seem right.

I helped with the morning drives and during lunch someone called the coon hunters to get the location of the carcass. Armed with the information I went straight to the place where the deer had fallen. There was a small caliber entry wound in its forehead.

The rack was smaller than I remembered, but a nice symmetrical eight point. My expanded bullet had struck him low in the right shoulder and broken his leg. The wound was almost as big as a quarter and did not look to have penetrated more than 4 or 5 inches. It was ugly and the odor was overpowering. Determined to honor the buck and remind myself of lessons learned, I took out my pruning saw and removed his scull plate and antlers.

The sweep of the main beams was an exact fit to the eight pointer I had poached back in 1975. I reckoned it to be evidence of the Maynard Hill genetics. It was my last hunt on the Maynard Hill. I miss it.

The Maynard Hill was learning ground for me and I will always hold that beautiful spot high in my memories. I learned a lot of lessons there—about deer, about men, about boys, about prayer, and about my faith. I learned the Would-be Woodsman had a long way to grow up in every aspect of my life.

I also learned a great lesson about humility and servant leadership in 1983. However, I didn't learn it well enough or quick enough. God let me struggle in the asphalt sealing swamp for a year. I had faced a test of spiritual maturity and failed it. God is a patient teacher. I would see that test again, and again.

Chapter 13

1984: Another Year of Big Changes

The year began on the heels of a beautiful white Christmas. It was cold enough for the snow to hang on through the New Year holiday. As Kathy and I discussed our future we knew the holding pattern we were in would not hold for much longer. We knew God was working in our lives but we still weren't sure about the direction. We decided to just keep doing what was in front of us and see what God would develop.

Kathy kept working at Springfield Lincoln Mercury and I did some odd jobs and substitute teaching while I was laid off from SASCO due to cold weather. At church, Kathy worked with Girls in Action and I poured myself into the music program. I interned myself to the music minister and learned a great deal about congregational worship and large scale musical/dramatic productions while assisting him.

The question about seminary would not go away. Jim Reimer encouraged me to look at Southwestern Baptist Theological Seminary in Fort Worth, Texas. I prepared an application for their Master of Music program but never mailed it. I was not sure why at the time.

My layoff did not last long as SASCO was building a new plant on a new site. They called me back to help with construction and remodeling of an unfinished house on the property to be used for company offices. Toward the end of the winter I made one more trip down home to attend Homer the Deerslayer's funeral. It was a sad day.

As the weather warmed the asphalt sealing business heated up. It was back to seven sunny days a week. At church we were gearing up for an Easter Passion play. I was chosen to sing and play the part of John, the beloved disciple. It was a life changing event for me as I experienced thoughts and emotions about my Lord and what He had done for me I had never considered before.

In the month leading up to Easter, my crew was responsible for skid-coat sealing every footpath at Silver Dollar City near Branson. We made the trip almost every day for a month. As spring approached the greening of the Ozarks awakened new life in me as I prepared my heart for the next—still unknown—step in our lives.

Part of the puzzle of our future became clear when Kathy's boss, Frank Hathcock, asked her to seriously consider moving to Joplin, Missouri, about an hour away, to take care of the books and run the office of his recently acquired Midwest Lincoln-Mercury-Jeep dealership. After talking and praying about it we agreed God was in it and she accepted the position, which was a great promotion and increase in income.

I worked for SASCO through the month of May and was glad to retire from the asphalt sealing business. Our move did not answer the question of the direction of my call to ministry but it did seem like a step forward, toward something.

Kathy found a nice house to rent in Joplin and I tested for the Joplin Fire Department. I did pretty well but could tell in the interview I was not going to be hired. As desperate as I was for employment, not being selected for a position I was well qualified for did not really bother me. Going back to the fire service did not feel right.

Kathy's task of straightening out the mired books at the dealership was going to be a monumental one so we decided I would play the part of *Mr. Mom* through the coming summer. I wasn't sure about the idea but was willing to do my part.

Family and friends came out to help us load a U-Haul truck with our furniture and stuff on Saturday of Memorial Day weekend. Kathy's brother Greg even made the trip with us to help unload it all in Joplin. It was an interesting house. One of the walls in the living room was covered with long shag carpeting—very interesting.

Our telephone would not be activated until after the holiday and this was still before the days of cell phones. We felt isolated as we settled down for the first night in our new home. Consequently, we were startled awake by the doorbell early Sunday morning. It was a state trooper who told Kathy of her father's heart attack. We loaded up Kathy's demo and headed back to Springfield.

Max was going to be all right after undergoing angioplasty, a relatively new procedure at the time. All through the months of June and July Kathy was responsible for the books of both dealerships since Max was the Office Manager of the Springfield store. We made many trips between Springfield and Joplin that summer. Kathy usually caught a much needed nap while I drove. The kids would fuss and/or sleep in the back seat.

The many hours behind the wheel of Kathy's demo allowed me time to think and pray about what was next for me. While the *Mr. Mom* summer seemed like limbo, I would not trade the experience for anything. Most men never come to understand the frustration of doing the same mundane tasks for their family over and over again. Most men never get to know their kids and learn their favorite clothes by washing them every other day, or sooner. Grocery shopping was a huge challenge for me but I learned to do it and even like it. I also learned to appreciate Kathy in ways I had never considered before.

The Would-be Woodsman could not be totally domesticated though and I practiced shooting my bow in the yard when Kathy was home. I took the children on outings which were just poorly camouflaged deer scouting expeditions. They didn't seem to mind too much although we did run into some toilet issues with the girls, especially Elizabeth.

Speaking of the toilet, that summer was Billy's time to be so trained. He picked it up very quickly and everyone was amazed a boy was so easy to potty train. There is much to be said for live demonstration in teaching. That's all I'm going to say about that.

It was also the summer the Olympics were held in Los Angeles. The kids and I watched many hours of gymnastics, swimming, diving, water polo, track and field, and of course, archery. We did have to take time out from our Olympic vigil to rush Billy to the emergency room for stitches in his head when he rolled off the picnic bench onto the concrete patio—another right-of-passage for Billy.

A dear friend asked me to do a concert of original music in his home in Springfield. Don Grove had been my Bible Study teacher at Second Baptist Church and had always found ways to encourage me in following after God. Thirty of Don's friends gathered in his great room as I shared the story of God's work in my life through songs I had written. Larry Ferguson accompanied me on the piano. Twenty years later my brother in law, Greg, presented me with compact disc of the recording he had made the night of the concert. Time does fly when you are having fun.

I was asked to be a lifeguard at Baptist Hill for the Greene County Baptist Association girls' week but they were out of cabin space. I borrowed my Grandma Freda's antique pop up camper and me and the kids really roughed it during camp. I remember they were bothered by the woods noise at night but adjusted to it before the week was done.

Kathy, of course, had to work but surprised us by coming to Baptist Hill on Thursday night. It was great to see her but it was especially great to see what she was driving—a white 1981 Datsun King Cab pickup with spoked chrome wheels. It was love at first sight, all over again. She wanted my approval before trading the yellow Lynx station wagon. I gladly gave it. The Would-be Woodsman rides again!

I received a call at camp from a friend at Second Baptist in Springfield. Mick Riddle's father was the pastor at First Baptist Church in Neosho, Missouri, and they were looking for an interim minister of music. He wanted permission to give his father my name and phone number. I gladly agreed.

The call from Rev. Leon Riddle came the next weekend and I was excited someone was interested in me, even for an interim position, for a couple of reasons. One, I have always worked for pay at something and while the *Mr. Mom* summer was really great, summer was just about over and it was time to get a job. Two, I had begun to wonder if God was ever going to use me in a church staff position again. Being quietly fired from my last position had not done much for my confidence in pastors, churches, or myself.

I met with Leon and some of the church members and began leading the choir and congregational singing on the last Sunday in August. The previous Minister of Music and Education had only held a bachelor's degree so I met the previous qualifications for the job. I had begun a personal study of religious education principles while at Second Baptist Church in Springfield. After officially meeting with the search committee things began to move quickly. We were living in Neosho by the end of September.

Life in a small, county seat town was a new experience for me but I loved it. Kathy had to drive 20 miles to work in Joplin every weekday and she hated it. Our children adjusted to small town life well and quickly thanks to new friends at a new church and an excellent school system. I think Neosho had a population of around ten thousand in those days and had won an All-America City award just before we moved there.

We rented an even nicer house on the north edge of town. There was a vacant lot next door I put to use as an archery range. It didn't take the Would-be Woodsman long to discover some nearby and open options for deer hunting. The first place that caught my eye was a 40 acre state-owned fire tower parcel outside of town near the intersection of Highway 86 and US Alternate 71.

Old Camp Crowder bordered Neosho on the south and there were many deer in accessible areas out there. I did not hunt on Camp Crowder the first year but spent all my spare time—which wasn't much—hunting around the Neosho fire tower. I hung my only portable tree stand in a corner of woods bordered by a power line cutover and an open field.

The first morning I was able to hunt early found me in the stand watching a nice buck reaching high for oak leafs from a tree across the field. The excitement and initial adrenalin wore off as the sun rose and the fog lifted. When he suddenly left that side of the field and came straight at me I was instantly recharged—actually overcharged. When the buck turned broadside at 25 yards I shot and missed badly.

I was still using my old Indian Stalker bow and my broadheads were sharp, I thought, but not sharp enough. Thinking back, I'm glad I missed the buck. Chances of recovering him (unless I missed my mark and hit his spine) were very slim. An underpowered bow and dull—less than razor sharp—broadheads are an unethical combination at best.

The next time I made it to my stand was an evening hunt and I was running a little late. When I reached my tree someone was already in it. I didn't know what to say. After introducing myself I said, "You're in my treestand." He replied, "No I'm not! This stand belongs to my friend John." My immediate thoughts were whoever John was, he was a liar. I didn't say it but did make my case and he climbed down and moved to another spot. We became good friends and hunted together on occasion.

One other incident comes to mind around the same stand location. On opening day of gun season I moved to my stand in the dark. I climbed the tree using my home-made climbing blocks which I had left on the tree. After hauling up my gun and gear, I settled into my home-made stand and seat. As I waited for it to get light I began to feel uneasy but didn't know why.

There were several trees near me with some across the fence line I was guarding. Looking at one of those trees, something didn't seem right. Suddenly, I saw movement up in the tree. This was some hunting excitement I had not bargained for. The movement was a human hand—a very white human hand. It was still dark but I began to focus on the shape of a man crouching and clinging to the fork of the tree not ten yards away.

He had beaten me to my spot and I was impressed because I get out real early. But I was not impressed enough to abandon my post. I had made previous preparations for this hunt from this spot and I was not going to leave. I thought about all the things I could say to make my argument but decided since we were both armed I should take an easier approach. I finally spoke up and said, "Good morning." He did not answer and I said nothing else.

It's pretty funny looking back at this event. There you had two stubborn Missourians facing each other in the dark, 12 feet off the ground in opposing trees with loaded rifles. As it grew light, he climbed down and moved off to the east. The strangest thing about him is he was wearing white gloves. That's a death wish in the deer woods. Even though I didn't even see a deer all day I felt I had won the strange duel in the woods.

Thanksgiving morning found me with my bow in same tree watching bucks and does chasing in the open field. A buck and doe worked through the woods behind me and I tried a 40 yard shot at the six pointer and missed again. I left the tree at 8:30, retrieved my arrow, went home, and drove the family to Springfield for double Thanksgiving dinners with both our families. That sounds like four meals; it felt like it.

In December I was very busy at the church but managed to get out to the fire tower for some short hunts. One morning I was still hunting through the middle of the 40 acre woods when I noticed movement behind me. It was a doe slipping through the brush. When she stepped into an opening at about 25 yards I let my arrow fly.

She took off in a big hurry and hit the power line clearing headed south toward my favorite corner. I went to the place where she had been standing when I released. The shot sounded like it had hit her but there was no blood. Her hoof prints were obvious even for a little distance down the power line trail. When the trail forked I lost hers. I looked for sign for several hours, eventually resorting to removing the leaves in line with where she and I had been standing. No arrow was there to be found.

Sickened by my blunder I sat down to figure out where I had gone wrong. I was pretty certain I had hit her with my arrow. I knew my bow was underpowered. It was supposed to have a 50 pound draw weight but I had checked it with a scale and it actually required only 43 pounds of pull. It was legal for hunting but just barely.

I had also come to believe my broadheads were inadequate. They were, I decided, dull and the design on-the-cheap made them difficult to sharpen. I should not have been hunting with them even though I could not afford better at the time.

My theory is my choice to hunt with this combination (weak bow and dull broadhead) caused my slow moving arrow to poorly penetrate without slicing the hide which would explain why there was no blood trail. I caused the deer to suffer a slow, painful death.

My treestand-squatting friend later told me he had seen a doe acting strangely between where I lost her and the corner. While scouting toward the end of the following summer I found what I assume were the bones of the doe. Who knows? There was one thing for certain—it was time to retire the Indian Stalker. I did, with one exception I will tell about later. Let me back up for a moment.

Our rented house in Neosho had two wood burning stoves—one in the den and one in the solarium. I needed firewood so I borrowed a chain saw and went to the State Forester and purchased a permit to gather firewood from timber tops in a state forest down near the Arkansas line. This turned out to be quite an adventure and lesson for the Would-be Woodsman.

One Friday morning I set out down Highway 71. This was my first trip south of Neosho. The terrain was rugged and the trees were just beginning to turn. It was a beautiful day. I had met a semi-retired preacher who had sort of invited me to come to his place east of the Big Sugar Creek in Macdonald County and hunt. My plan was to cut a load of wood then make my round-about way toward his place and scout for deer sign.

I found the cutover forest with no problem and soon had my little truck's bed loaded with chunks of oak ready for the fire. When I left the State Forest entrance I turned east instead of back to the highway. Cutting firewood, though needed, was really just an excuse to go deer hunting without a bow or gun. We hunters call that scouting.

The paved road surface quickly gave way to gravel. As I proceeded down the road I began to notice water standing in the ditches and pools along the roadway. It had rained recently in Neosho but evidently much more rain had fallen to the south of us. I crossed a wet weather branch where the water was slightly over the concrete slab. A little further along, I encountered another slab—the water was a little higher.

I really wanted to see this place so I stubbornly pressed on. A few miles further I saw the road was partially covered with water. At first, the water was only on the left had side of the roadway. Anxiety was building in me but I refused to give in to my fear. I had set out on a mission and did not plan to be denied. I remember thinking out loud, "I've gone too far to turn back now."

As I continued to creep on down the road water continued to cover more and more of it. Soon it forced me over to the far right with my left tires wet in the ever deepening approaches to Big Sugar Creek. I knew I was getting close to my destination.

Finally with all four tires in water up to the rims, I stopped and had a conversation with myself and God. I was well aware of how foolish it would be to continue but I hated the thought of not succeeding. I thought, "I can't go back!" As I argued with myself I heard a still, small voice ask, "Why not? You have a reverse gear. That is an option, you know." After recognizing God's voice in my mind I decided His plan was better and backed out of my predicament.

My way too strong desire to scout a new place to hunt almost led me to disaster. As I drove home to Neosho I sensed I had turned a new corner in my spiritual life. I realized the Would-be Woodsman could not run the show and there are many things in life which are much more important than hunting. I had also put to rest a dangerous myth in my life. Sometimes you can go back to where you lost your way or your mind or your spiritual power and take a different path.

Chapter 14

1985: Life in the Flower Box City

The house we lived in had a double car garage but only the right side had a power door lift. It was Kathy's side. During the hectic pre-Easter season I came home one Wednesday evening a little later than Kathy and the kids.

Our trash pickup day was Thursday. Let me back up a second. We had no pets at the time but I had been getting flea bites, usually while in the dining room and kitchen area. One afternoon I had discovered a nasty looking, snaggle-toothed cat sitting on our back deck. When I stepped outside he ran under the deck, which was low to the ground. The kids eventually saw him too but I forbad them from touching the fleabag.

Another piece of this story was some critter had been ripping open the trash bags in the garage when Kathy would forget to close her garage door, which was pretty often. Another piece of evidence in my defense is I had been finding songbird feathers near and around my two bird feeders.

Getting back to the story. My day had been a long one with a rough finish during Easter program choir rehearsal. When I got home I parked in front of my garage door with the motor running. When I lifted the door I saw five or six trash bags ripped open and scattered across my stall. The culprit was still there. The snaggle-toothed tomcat made his break through Kathy's open stall door and disappeared into the night.

As I tracked the cat running out the door my eyes fell on my Indian

Stalker bow and quiver hanging on the wall. In a mad rush I took down the bow and quickly mounted an arrow to the string. I stepped around the corner of the house and spied the cat crouching in the strip of white gravel which ran along the full length of the chain-linked fence.

I drew the bow and fired instinctively and heard the arrow strike the gravel. The cat ran along the fence into the deeper darkness of the neighbor's back yard. Kathy met me as I entered the house. She asked, "What were you doing in the garage so long?" I said, "I was cleaning up the mess that stupid cat made because you left the garage door open again." I should have stopped right there but foolishly added, "He won't be back for a while."

With a fire in her eyes only a wife can direct at her husband she asked, "What did you do to that cat?" I knew I had messed up but had to confess, "I shot an arrow at it, but I missed. It sure took off in a hurry though." I spent the next ten minutes responding to more piercing looks and making my case, trying to put as much blame on her as possible. It was ugly. The kids were in bed and I didn't think about them overhearing our not too gentle conversation.

The next morning was trash day. Kathy had already left for work and while the kids were getting their coats and things I took out the re-bagged trash and decided I would take a quick look out back and retrieve my arrow. It was plain to see where the arrow struck the gravel so I headed down the slope along the fence. I searched the entire length of the fence and was puzzled I could not find the arrow. As I turned and started back up toward the house something caught my attention out of the corner of my left eye.

My arrow was pointing to the bright blue February sky. The snaggle-toothed tomcat—frozen in a sprinting pose—was skewered on the end of it. I panicked. What would the neighbors think of me? What if word got around to the people at church? I moved quickly and carried the dead cat, with arrow still attached, to the front driveway.

As I was placing the evidence in a trash bag to be hauled away with the others my children came out into the garage. It was time to take them to school. Nervously I said, "Don't come out here kids, I've got to take care of something." Amy replied with a scolding edge to her voice,

"What did you do Daddy, kill the cat?" I knew immediately they had overheard the previous evening's parental conversation.

This really sent me into an emotional spin. What would my kids think of me? I tried to explain what I had done and why. It sounded feeble and lame as I spoke it. I was some relieved when the girls said they wanted to see the dead cat. Billy was quiet.

We loaded up in the Datsun with the girls in the jump seats and Billy in his car seat in the front (it used to be legal). Billy's daycare was at Abundant Life Assembly of God Church, less than a half mile away. As we drove I pleaded with my children not to tell anyone about my cat killing spree. People just wouldn't understand. By this time I, myself, didn't understand why I had done the deed.

When we pulled into the church parking lot I knew something was wrong. Billy would usually give me a kiss before I took him in the building. He wouldn't even look at me. He just sat there. I pleaded, "What's the matter Billy?" He answered with quivering lip and teary eyes, "I like cats, you know." My heart was broken and my eyes teared up too. I begged his forgiveness and made one more plea for him not to mention it to anyone at school.

I carried the terribly sad little boy to the doors of the daycare. As soon as I touched the door to go in I sensed a change in Billy. He sucked in a deep breath as I opened the door and shouted loudly with pride only a son can have for his father, "Hey teacher! My daddy killed a cat." " Oh no!" I thought, "I'm busted. The cat is really out of the bag." The daycare director simply smiled and said, "Mr. West, would you like to come to my house?"

Our Easter production was a collection of Gaither music we embellished with first century costumes and drama sets. It was a lot of work and a lot of fun. My plan was to build some backdrops and costumes which we could use in larger productions in the coming years.

We bought a tri-level house in the spring on the corner of Benton and Joplin Streets in Neosho. It was located on the hill above the U. S. Fish and Wildlife Service hatchery. The kids and I spent many hours feeding the millions of trout in various stages of growth. It was cheap entertainment and made for fun memories.

I loved that house. It was situated near the homes of several of the church members and our friends. Neosho was small enough so every location was close to whatever you needed. Joplin Street ran east and west. It was a fantastic sledding hill.

There was an event during the spring which challenged my emotional health. I was home early one afternoon with the flu or something. The television was on a local station while I lay coasting on the couch in the downstairs den. Programming was interrupted to report on the shooting of two Missouri State Highway Patrolmen near Branson. One was very seriously injured.

A news crew on the scene captured the loading of the seriously injured patrolman into an air ambulance. I recognized him—Jimmie Linegar. The last time I had seen him was back in 1984 as I was leaving Silver Dollar City at the end of a long asphalt sealing day.

He was out of his patrol car directing traffic. My heart had swelled with pride because I knew him. I wanted to speak to him and tell him I had finally graduated from college. It was not possible in that setting plus I realized my job supervising an asphalt sealing crew didn't exactly look like success.

The first time I had seen Jimmie was at a spring concert at Central High School in 1969. He was in my sister Theresa's class. He was a sophomore and I was in the eighth grade at Pipkin Junior High School. My sister was in the Concert Choir. Jimmie was a percussionist in the orchestra. He really looked cool playing the timpani.

My next encounter with Jimmie was the following spring when I barely made the Central varsity baseball team as a freshman. Most upper classmen gave freshman players a hard time. Jimmie was not like that. He was friendly and encouraging.

I admired him and wanted to emulate his way of living life. I watched him closely. He was a good student, a fine athlete, and an accomplished musician with a ready smile. I did not realize he was my high school hero until he died. He never knew he inspired me to be more than most people (including myself) thought I could become.

The design of the protective vest worn by our troopers in those days did not cover them on the sides. At a routine traffic road block, a white supremacist had opened up on Jimmie with an Uzi machine gun at point blank range. The energy from the multiple impacts on the left side of his chest turned him to expose his right side.

News of Jimmie's murder pained me more deeply than I had ever felt before. I wanted to go to his funeral which was held in the Williams Memorial Chapel at the School of the Ozarks. My boss and pastor refused my request for time off to attend. His refusal hurt me deeply. I struggled for years with forgiving Leon for denying me an opportunity to act on my grief.

Leon was really well thought of by most of the people at First Baptist. He was famous and loved for twelve minute sermons. We always beat the Methodist to the restaurants. Despite his many wonderful attributes and winning smile he was not good at communicating with his staff. He wounded me on several occasions and I failed once again God's test of spiritual maturity. I cried to others instead of God.

One week during the summer our kids were in Springfield with their grandparents. Kathy was very busy with her work. I was invited by Don Grove and two of our friends to join them on a three-day fast and prayer retreat on Truman Lake. I was only able to join them for two days but I began my fast when they did.

When I arrived at the lake they were concentrating their prayers for people we knew who were struggling with relationships and life. We prayed and sang and read the scriptures together. It was a pretty sweet experience for me.

On the morning of our last day together the focus of our prayers became each other. Each man spontaneously confessed fears, concerns and sins. I really began to feel the movement of the Holy Spirit in power.

I took this opportunity to ask my brothers to pray that my call to ministry would become clear. I confessed I had felt called to preach God's word when I was a teenager but had become confused about it. They challenged me to explain my thinking. One of them said, "Wayne, if you believe God called you to preach, what is the problem?"

They helped me identify two arguments I had held in my heart for a long time but never expressed. One was I thought God had called me to preach when I was fourteen years old. I actually and truly received

Christ as my Savior when I was sixteen. My dilemma was I didn't know if God could or would call a person to serve Him before they were born again.

My other problem was I simply did not feel worthy to be used by God to preach His word. When my friends pressed me I told them my doubts and self-loathing tracked back to a couple of events early in my marriage. I had very nearly broken my marriage vows and left Kathy for other women on two separate occasions.

One of my Christian brothers asked me very bluntly if I had asked God's forgiveness for my sins. I replied I had sincerely done so. Neal reminded me if I had sought forgiveness, God had given it, according to His promise and character. Someone asked me if Kathy had forgiven me—she had.

Neal kept the pressure up, "Wayne, what is your problem?" I blurted out, "God and Kathy may be able to forgive me but I can't forgive myself!" Neal stepped close and buried the tip of his index finger into my chest and said, "Who do you think you are? If God can forgive you and you refuse to forgive yourself, you elevate yourself above him. I don't know the answer to your timing question but I can tell you—worthy— (emphasized with his finger again) has nothing to do with your call. If we had to be worthy, we couldn't even be saved. What matters is that we are usable and willing." I began to weep as my brothers gathered around me and placed their hands on my head and shoulders. I felt as if a great burden had been lifted from my soul.

The next Saturday Kathy and I traveled to Springfield to collect our children. I dozed in the front porch swing while waiting for supper to be prepared at Kathy's parents. In the lazy, hazy place between sleep and awake I heard the words of Jeremiah the prophet, "The word of the Lord came to me saying, 'Before I formed you in the womb I knew you, before you were born I set you apart; I appointed you as a prophet to the nations.'" (Jeremiah 1:4-5)

I came immediately awake and prayed, "I hear you Father. You can call anyone you want, any time you want. Forgive me for dragging my feet. I will serve you." On the way home I shared my experience and thoughts with Kathy and she agreed we should move forward.

My application and acceptance to Midwestern Baptist Theological Seminary was still active. Within a matter of weeks I was commuting to Springfield on a Monday morning to begin my seminary journey in a satellite classroom. It was scary but I soon discovered the truth—with God's help, I could do it.

Kathy got us a good deal on a new commuter car at her dealership. It was a bare bones 1985 beige Lynx. She had them add air conditioning, a stereo with cassette player, and cruise control. We named it Sandy. I hated to give up the Datsun King Cab but we sold it to my friend Mitch Wright for his son Brian.

Archery season opened on the first of October as usual but the Would-be Woodsman had other things on his mind. My busy ministry and my academic challenges greatly curtailed my time in the woods. I don't remember even seeing a deer while afield with either gun or bow.

I do remember one precious moment and one significant decision. The precious moment involved Billy, who was three years old. He had been after me to take him hunting but I had resisted, knowing if I did it would probably be an unsuccessful trip. My time in the woods was limited and I was hoping for a chance to harvest a deer. I have never been able to say "no" to my children for very long, unless the request involved something I saw as hurtful to them. One Friday evening Billy asked again and I relented.

Billy was wide awake the next morning as we left the house for the short trip to the fire tower woods. It was the early bow season and I carried the old Indian stalker, a home-made tree seat, and Billy (part of the way) through the darkness to a spot overlooking a small pond.

After attaching the seat to a tree I sat down and held Billy on my lap. He was fading fast as the gray light began to show in the eastern sky. A fine mist began to fall. I wrapped Billy in my field jacket and laid him on the ground beneath the seat. My legs protected him from the mist.

As I sat there I realized there was not much chance I would score as a hunter but I felt very successful as a dad and nothing else mattered. The Would-be Woodsman had learned a great lesson. Hunting success can be defined in many ways. I would not trade a world record buck for the two hours I watched over Billy as he slept—warm and comfortable in the misty rain.

The significant decision involved my Remington 742, 30-06. Not long after I started working full time at First Baptist Church I began to have a very troubling and recurring dream. The dream setting was always the same. I am out hunting with my rifle and see deer running toward me. As they get closer I realize they are people running like deer.

As they get even closer I recognize they are people I know. I get excited, just like when I am encountering deer in the woods. My heartbeat races and my mind tunes out everything else. I am conflicted. I know I shouldn't shoot but I am out of control. I want to shoot and finally do.

As I approach the downed game (person) it is always someone from my life at church; past or present. It was usually someone who exercised some power over my work, which was a huge part of my life. It was usually a deacon or the chairman of finance. Sometimes it was my pastor. My remorse would be so gut-wrenchingly strong I would wake up feeling sick and drenched with sweat.

In one such dream my trophy was a man who controlled the finances of the church. In the dream I voiced my deep sorrow and asked his forgiveness. While bleeding out, he looked up and smiled as he said, "It's all right Brother Wayne. It's OK." I fought myself awake, sickened and covered with moisture. The words of an evangelist I respected came to mind as I tried to calm down. He had said, "If you own something and it is giving you grief, get rid of it."

I was uncomfortable with how easy it was to make multiple shots with the semi-automatic firearm—faster than my brain could think them through. I realize now the gun was not my problem. The real problem was my frustration and resistance to those who wielded real or imagined control over my work. The frustration and anxiety I could not even talk about was coming to the surface in my subconscious dreaming. However, when I decided to sell my gun to our youth minister and purchased a new compound bow and accessories, the dreams went away.

Chapter 15

1986: Life on the Road

Once I had it settled that my call to ministry would involve preaching I began to dream about the possibility of becoming an Air Force chaplain. With family, the church, and school going full blast there was plenty to occupy my time and thoughts. But as the New Year began, this seed of possibility—the Air Force Chaplaincy—often surfaced from the depths of my mind.

I had made friends with three other seminary students who were driving to Springfield from the Joplin area. One was the associate pastor of a sister Baptist church in Joplin. Another student was the minister of education at a Baptist church in Miami, Oklahoma. We would also stop in Sarcoxie and pick up the pastor of the Southern Baptist church there.

We not only shared the expenses of the commute but we became a very effective study team. Our professors would provide us a study guide for tests and we would divide up the questions then meet a few days later in Joplin. Each of us would concentrate on writing the most detailed response we could and bring copies for everyone to the meeting, which usually involved lunch. This was good stewardship of our limited time. I learned a lot from these bright men.

The year's First Baptist Church Easter musical project was the biggest production I ever directed. The year Kathy and I were married we taught a youth class on Sunday evenings at Northwest Baptist Church. One of the energetic young men in the junior high group was

Pat Edmonds. He grew up to be a fine actor and director who played an instrumental role in founding the Stained Glass Theatre in Springfield.

Early in the year I mentioned to him my desire to do a passion play, which would be a huge challenge for a church of our size. Pat perked up with interest and shared with me his desire to write and direct a passion play. I selected the music to build the dialogue around and we both went to work.

By the time Easter rolled around our worship room was transformed. We had built a mountain over the grand piano and a temple/palace set over the organ. Many rehearsals had developed a cast of sixty from all age groups. The costumes were completed and spectacular, thanks to Mrs. Marble who was not even a member of the church. Pat used his connections and helped us rent and set up theatre lights and controls. It was a huge production depicting the last days of Jesus' life through His resurrection.

It was a great deal of work for everyone involved. We performed the play several times. One anxious moment came as we approached the Saturday evening performance. Pat had to stay in Springfield for some good reason and had detailed one of his Stained Glass crew to run the light cues. When it was time to begin, he had not arrived. I asked God to help me know what to do.

One of our church members was running a follow spotlight from the balcony. I gave him instructions to focus the spot tight on any dialogue or solo and open it wide at all other times. Pastor Riddle made the opening greeting and led in prayer. When he said, "Amen," the appropriate lights came on. The drama tech had arrived during the prayer.

When May came to a close so did my first year of seminary. I had completed 16 credit hours—what a full time student would normally do in a semester. My grades had been good. The only B I remember was from Dr. Hulitt Gloer for my work in Synoptic Gospels. I was pleased with my GPA, which I took as evidence I could do the work. I was equally discouraged with how long the Master of Divinity degree would take going to school only part-time.

In early August we took a family vacation. Kathy's employer

maintained a customized van in demo service and encouraged his managers to take it on vacations. He even paid for the first tanks of fuel. Kathy's brother, Jeff, was living and working in the Washington D. C. area. He and his wife, Terry, invited us to stay with them for a week or so. They had two boys near the age of our girls and had just adopted two young girls from Korea. We were anxious to meet them.

As we planned the trip we decided we could save a lot of money if we would drive straight through. The rear seat of the customized van folded down to a bed and there was a television for the children to watch. We could make the trip without lodging expenses.

I remember we stopped briefly in St. Louis to visit a young lady from church who was having a surgery there. I refilled one of the fuel tanks during that stop which turned out to be a huge problem. We drove on through the night and into the next day. Sometime after midnight Kathy relieved me as driver until morning.

We saw a bear get hit by a car while it was crossing the road in western Pennsylvania which roused my Would-be-Woodsman blood. When we arrived at Gettysburg in the afternoon Kathy suggested we kill some time there and wait until the D. C. traffic settled down before trying to find Jeff and Terry's Silver Spring, Maryland, apartment. I was very impressed with the battle park.

The Washington D. C. traffic was overwhelming. Maneuvering an oversized Ford van through it was challenging, to say the least. It was really good to see Jeff and his family. We had not seen them in quite a while. Their new daughters were gorgeous and the boys were always fun.

Our first trip into the city was on the train. It was an impressive adventure for all of us hillbillies. We purchased a bus tour package and took in every museum and memorial we could. I did not make the Vietnam Memorial or Washington monument on the first day.

I will never forget my first encounter with the Vietnam War Memorial. One evening Jeff took Kathy and me downtown just as the sun was setting. The memorial was unbelievably moving in the fading light. We could see our reflection in the marble wings and the bronze statues of the soldiers seemed ready to come alive and speak to me.

We had been to the Lincoln Memorial with the kids in daylight and it was impressive. It was even more so when we experienced in the evening. Having a little more time and less responsibility allowed me to carefully read President Lincoln's second inaugural address. The depth of his spirituality moved me to leak a little.

The last stop on our evening tour by Jeff was the Washington Monument. The line was long but Jeff insisted it would be worth the wait. He was right, as usual (except about night driving). The night-time view from the top was more than spectacular.

While we were waiting for over an hour in line I could not keep my eyes from tracking back to an Air Force officer in his class B uniform. My insipient, nagging desire to once again wear an Air Force uniform (one with officer insignia on the shoulders) broke through to the surface on the spot. The whole trip, starting with Gettysburg, red-lined my patriot meter.

Both families piled into the van for a two-day trip to the beach at Wildwood, New Jersey. We rented rooms just off the boardwalk and spent the afternoon on the beach. The kids enjoyed playing with their cousins in the edge of the water and making sand castles.

As I lay sandwiched between the sun-warmed sand and cool, salt-scented breeze, I experienced a deep and restful peace. My desire to be a spiritual man and a patriot came into balance there. I kept those thoughts to myself until we were well on our way home but I felt it was time to step out and move on with my education and quest to become an Air Force chaplain.

After dinner, we took both families to play on the boardwalk. The most fun ride was a giant Ferris wheel. I remember being high in the night sky with our new nieces, Holly and Wendy.

The van kept stalling in traffic as we were making our way back to Silver Spring the following day. I tried everything, even switching fuel tanks. We finally made it home and called the nearest Ford dealership. No source of the problem could be found even after a day in the shop.

The van kept dying as we continued our sightseeing around the D.C. area. It finally dawned on me it always happened when running on tank number one. I had not added fuel to that tank since St. Louis. I must have bought some bad gas.

We took the kids to the Washington Mall one more time before we left. Driving around the area was confusing and frustrating to me. The use of certain lanes changed with the traffic day. We were trying to get to the parking lot by the Washington Monument and I found myself at a stop light in a lane which required me to turn right a block short of my destination.

When the light changed I punched the accelerator and went straight ahead. Just as I was thinking I had made a slick move a D.C. traffic policeman stepped out from behind a bush and motioned for me to stop. My heart was pounding and I was embarrassed. The officer was kind but plainly pointed out the danger of my slick move.

He took my license back to his motorcycle. When he returned with the ticket he lingered and acted as if he had something else to say. He finally left us with well wishes. We parked in the desired lot and as I studied my ticket, I glanced at my drivers' license. I was shocked to realize it had expired on my birthday, which had taken place on the trip.

Up until that moment I had harbored hard feelings toward the officer. I had felt he was just picking on me—an obvious tourist. My thoughts about him quickly became thoughts of gratitude and appreciation when I realized he could have made it very hard for me to get home.

After we said our good-byes to Jeff and his family we headed south. We took a different route through Virginia, Tennessee, and Kentucky to get back home to Missouri. Once on the open highway I was able to burn the bad gas out of tank number one. Kathy and I talked about our future on the long drive home.

By the time we made it back to Neosho we had decided to resign from my job at First Baptist Church and move to Carl Junction. Kathy would keep her job and Carl Junction would put us in a great school system—close enough to get to the kids from her work if they needed her. I would commute to Kansas City each week.

We put our house on the market and listed it with a friend from church. A contract quickly developed and we moved to a rental house near Carl Junction, just north of Joplin. Not long after we moved and

I began commuting the closing date was cancelled and the deal fell through.

It turned out the deal was hopeless from the start and involved the buyer letting his government loan lapse so he could buy our house. They were planning to finance through another government program which rejected the sale. Imagine that! I was disappointed in our friend and angry at the owner of the real estate company. I told him what I thought and cancelled my contract to list with his company. We found a renter fairly quickly and began a long and worrisome ordeal for me as a landlord.

Kathy was great through all of this turmoil. She enrolled the kids in school, found childcare just two blocks from our house, and accomplished a million other things needing to be done. I packed a week's worth of clothes and stuff into Sandy and headed north into the unknown galaxy of Kansas City, Missouri.

Classes were Tuesday through Friday so I would leave on Monday evening and return on Friday evening each week. It was about 200 miles each way. The first week on campus started early and was filled with testing, paperwork, and orientation. I would be staying in the dorm on campus. The first week was tough, being in a strange place and not knowing anyone. I quickly discovered two friends from my Tatum Chapel days. Bob Lilley and his brother-in-law Mike Cook were in their third year. It was nice to know someone there even though they were very busy.

The administration sponsored a mixer and picnic one evening but I did not go. Instead, I pulled a portable archery target (burlap bag stuffed with foam rubber) out of the hatchback and started practicing with my bow in the edge of the woods next to the dorm parking lot. As I was launching my arrows, a man about my age with a daughter about Elizabeth's age spoke to me while they walked across the parking lot toward the mixer.

He stopped and talked some more on their return. His name was Darrell Smith and we had several things in common besides being married Baptist preachers beginning seminary in a strange big city. We both thought we would have to give up hunting when we started seminary but were having second thoughts. I had already checked out some local conservation land and Darrell said he was preaching in an open-country church about an hour north which had some hunting possibilities. It looked like our friendship had some possibilities as well.

Darrell's wife was Janice, his son Philip, and his daughter Mary. I enjoyed them all immensely as they helped me with my weekly homesickness. Their life was full of busyness and stress like every other seminary family but their door was always open to me. I tried not to wear out my welcome but I'm sure I did some.

Our classes were spaced in eight week sessions so the study pace was pretty hectic. Darrell and I managed to shoot our bows, scout for deer, and keep on top of our studies. One evening while hanging around with the Smith's, Janice squared off with Darrell and asked him, "Did you tell Wayne?" It was obvious they had previously discussed something. Darrell took a deep breath, looked at me, and told me a story.

The previous year Darrell had been pastor of Sopchoppy Baptist Church in north Florida. One afternoon while heading into one of his remote hunting areas he met a game warden friend on his way out. After their visit Darrell parked his truck but before he could get out he began to have some strange sensations—numbness, loss of motor control, and fading consciousness. He said he remembered slumping forward on the horn. His next realization was being flown out of the bush in an air ambulance.

I hung on every word of his slow developing story. He explained Janice wanted me to know about his potential health issues. I was hungry to have a friend and saw this as a chance to be one. I told her Darrell's medical history was not a problem for me and I would be glad to watch out for him.

We talked each other into skipping class to hunt opening morning of the archery season on the Platte River Wildlife Area about 20 minutes from campus. We drove Darrell's old Ford pickup which he described as church basement green. It was a good thing we were excited and left early because just as we turned into the parking area I remembered I had left my archery release in my car.

It was just getting light as we turned into the area for the second time. We had started down a graveled forest road when Darrell stopped the truck. I gave him a look that said, "What's up?" He said, "I'm sorry man but I've got to go." With that he hopped out and disappeared into the woods. It was the first of many such time outs for us in the years to come. It seems the mere presence of trees in the woods would act upon Darrell with the swiftness of Turbolax. After he talked me out of half of my bandanna a couple of times I always carried toilet paper for Darrell—and me.

Another interesting thing about my friend was he dipped snuff when we were out and about. I had been around Baptist churches and missions most of my life and had never met an ordained minister who smoked, chewed, or dipped—at least around me. I quickly learned smokeless tobacco was allowed for preachers in the deep south, as long as you didn't bring your spit cup into the pulpit. I was learning a lot in seminary.

Darrell was called to be the pastor at Alta Vista Baptist church near the Davies and DeKalb county line. He had been invited to hunt on some land near the church and managed to get the invitation extended to me also. We made an afternoon trip to check out some woods and were really impressed. There was a thick 15 acre piece of woods bordered on the north by an alfalfa field and a large milo crop. South, across the road was a huge field of standing corn. A good portion of the woods was locust and bois d'arc trees.

I found a tree I liked a hundred yards south of the alfalfa field. Several game trails converged in the vicinity. It was the best tree to hang my home made stand and seat in. However, it was a locust tree with thousands of scary long thorns. I was determined and removed all the thorns from the trunk with a folding pruning saw I had borrowed from my father-in-law several years before (he never asked for it back that I recall).

I was invited by a fellow seminary student to lead music in a series of revival meetings in his church in Hamilton, Missouri. This town was not too far from Darrell's church. We would pass the Hamilton exit on I-35 and sometimes stop there at the McDonalds. The revival would start on Sunday, the second day of November. Kathy and I had decided it would be best if I stayed in Kansas City for the weekend.

With the green light on, Darrell and I began to plan a camping and hunting adventure for the Friday night and Saturday before the revival started. We would leave campus as soon as my Hebrew class ended on Friday, drive north to a state park, rent a camping site, and set up Darrell's tent. It sounded like a good plan.

On Tuesday morning of the last week of October I met Darrell in the small campus cafeteria. He said, "Man I messed you up." He loved to start a conversation like that. He explained he had found what he thought was a better spot for my stand. He decided to do me a favor and move it. He further explained, "I was carrying your stand and stuff through the woods when I found the biggest scrape I have ever seen. It is six feet long and three feet wide and not 30 yards from your tree."

I exclaimed, "Why did you move my stand?" He said, "I didn't know it was there until I had already taken your stand down. I'm sorry man. I didn't hang the stand, it's in the back of my truck." He made some other comment about my choosing a black locust tree for a perch. All week long I made plans for sneaking back in there and hanging my stand. Such planning may have distracted me from my studies.

It was a hard week. As the weekend approached I began to feel stressed. I was in my second term of Hebrew and translation was getting more challenging. I stressed about home when it dawned on me I would not see Kathy and the kids until the following Friday evening. I felt stressed about hunting. I had been an unsuccessful bow hunter since 1978. The pressure was on me to produce.

I was tempted to skip all my classes Friday but I knew Kathy was sacrificing a lot for me to go to seminary and it wouldn't be right or fair. Besides, I could not afford to get behind in Hebrew. I love the language but Dr. Matheny added a twisted layer to the course. He had been known around campus for years as Meany Matheny. He was proud of the title.

His class would be my last for the week. I was ready to escape to the woods when Dr. Matheny jolted me out of a daydream by calling on me to read my translation assignment to the class. About halfway through the passage he shouted "No!" Maybe he didn't scream but it sounded like it to me. "How in the world did you ever come up with that? That's ridiculous!" he added. I was so shaken I could not explain or answer in any way.

I pulled back within myself and simmered through the rest of the class. My gear and clothes were already loaded in my car and I drove to Darrell's apartment in campus housing. He had the church basement green Ford ready to go. I lead us out of Gladstone and onto the interstate.

Thirty miles up the pike I noticed Darrell's flashing headlights in my rear view mirror. I took the next exit and pulled into a truck stop. Darrell needed fuel and while he was filling he asked, "What happened back there Wayne?" I let a blast of air escape from my lungs (a trait I had picked up from my father) and replied, "How did you know?" "You're driving like a mad man," he responded, "You're going to run my old truck into the ground. What is it?" I told him about my humiliation by Meany Matheny. He sagely advised, "Forget it man. You'll be done with him in a month. Let's go hunting'." I let Darrell lead the rest of the way.

After setting up our camp site in the state park I changed into my hunting clothes I had laundered in baking soda the evening before. We parked his truck at a church member's place adjacent to the fifteen acre woodlot. Darrell described where his lean-up, two-by-four stand was located. It was maybe 150 yards into the woods from the truck.

I headed north hauling my stand, bow, and daypack. Moving slowly to avoid sweating was tough. I could feel the daylight slipping away. I turned east when I hit the tractor road running between the woods and the alfalfa plot and crept along until I was due north of the tree. With the wind in my face I slipped over an old fence and made my way to the spot. I expected to hear a snort or see a bounding flag with every step.

Once I made it to the tree I fastened on my climbing blocks and re-hung the stand where I had placed it a couple of weeks before. As I felt sweat break out and trickle down my neck and back my thoughts about Darrell were not particularly friendly.

It was nearly 4:00 when I settled into place facing east on my stand. I began to relax and talk to God. I told Him about the pressure I was feeling from so many fronts. As I remembered Philippians 4:6-7 and prayed things started to change. I began to notice what a beautiful day it was. It was perfect weather for hunting. I was only a few hundred yards from the best friend I had ever made.

I mentioned to the Lord how I had been hunting with a bow for seven years without harvesting a deer and how I was willing to shoot the first deer to come by. I even made some comical statement about my needing to prove my credibility as a woodsman because Kathy was probably wondering where I was really spending my time.

The antlers from the prayer buck of 1983 were hanging next to my stand. My plan was to remain quiet until 4:45 then try my hand at rattling. I had never tried it before. As I was waiting and listening I remembered it was Halloween. I had always enjoyed it as a boy and was finally beginning to enjoy this day.

I hung my bow and picked up the antlers when my watch indicated it was time. After tucking my release under the cuff of my sleeve I started a sequence of rattling. Immediately I sensed motion back to my right and turned to see a deer hustling up the trail and looking for trouble.

The antlers continued to rattle as I hung them on a peg. By the time I picked up my bow and attached the release to the string the four point buck passed my tree and stopped. There was no hesitation. I drew and released the arrow. I saw and heard it strike back of the buck's left shoulder.

He ran to the northeast and I saw the arrow shaft and fletchings vibrate with every bound. He passed between two trees and quickly disappeared. I may have heard him fall but by then I had lost my mind. I tried to catch my breath and calm down. After sliding out of my stand I tried to be quiet as I approached the two trees. The aluminum arrow shaft had snapped off on the left tree.

I picked up the piece of arrow and made my way to where I thought I would find Darrell. Hearing a soft whistle I turned to see Darrell looking down at me. "You killed a deer, didn't you?" he said with a big smile. I replied I had shot one and probably killed it.

We made our way back to the truck to collect a couple of flashlights.

The church member joined us on our now moonlit search. We found the two trees easy enough and found blood but not much. I began to get anxious when the easy blood trail petered out quickly.

Darrell was much more experienced at trailing wounded animals and was able to settle me down. With his encouragement we both went to our hands and knees and began to find a micro-trail of pinhead-sized droplets. Darrell's other friend began to make circles around us without a flashlight as we were concentrating on this painstaking task. The moonlight had become brilliant as full darkness descended.

While Darrell and I were making miniscule progress with every tiny drop our helper began to make slow sweeps across the general line ahead of our trail. I was really glad and relieved when I heard him say, "Here he is. I see his white belly in the moonlight." The deer was only thirty yards beyond our location.

When we got to the buck the finder commented, "I thought you said he was a forked horn." It had happened pretty fast and four points was all I had time to verify. I sheepishly made my excuse. Darrell came to my defense pointing out it was a mistake easily made considering the size of the deer. The oversized body made the pretty nice six point rack look small.

The rest of the evening passed in fuzzy warm satisfaction for me. By the time we finally settled into our sleeping bags I was exhausted but too keyed up to sleep. Darrell read aloud "The Jersey Devil" chapter from Tom Brown's *The Tracker*. Before we drifted off to sleep Darrell said a couple of things I will never forget.

The first was, "There are a lot of people who would like to do what you accomplished today." The final thought for the day was, "Wayne, I'm really happy that you killed that buck but I gotta be honest. I wish it had been me."

When we delivered the six pointer to a meat processor in Hamilton the next morning the man applied its dressed weight to a live weight chart. My little buck probably weighed 250 pounds on the hoof.

When I finally got home the following Friday night it felt so good to be there. I had missed Kathy, Amy, Elizabeth, and Billy terribly over the two week period. On Saturday morning I took Billy outside and showed him the antlers and head of my deer. He was impressed and proud of his dad. I cherish a picture Kathy took of us posing with the buck head and cape; if I could only find it.

That was about all for the Would-be Woodsman in 1986 with a couple of exceptions. Back in the summer I had applied for an antlerless deer permit for the area around the State Forest near the town of Mindenmines, Missouri. It was known to locals as the Tree Farm. The drawing had been favorable to me for the first time. I stopped on my way home the only Friday afternoon of the Missouri gun season.

This area was a reclaimed strip mine network of pits and dumps planted in many species of coniferous trees. In the last hour of the hunting day I slipped into a spot overlooking a pit filled with water. Just as I was getting ready to call it quits a doe moved down to the pond edge to drink, 40 yards opposite of my position.

I made a quick decision. It was close to the end of legal shooting time—a track in the dark would be difficult. I was not sure my position was actually on the State Forest property. I was close to the boundary. The doe was possibly, if not probably, beyond it. There was venison in the freezer at home so I passed up the shot. As I drove the rest of the way home it dawned on me I had—for the first time—passed up the opportunity to harvest a deer. A corner had been turned in my development as the Would-be Woodsman.

The final piece to a pretty fine year was my selection by the Home Mission Board for entrance into the Air Force Chaplain Candidate program. The year of 1986 had been full of change and surprise. God had been good to us, as always.

Chapter 16

1987: Near Miss in the Woods

This year jumped off with a January term at seminary. Every Master of Divinity student was required to complete a course of Clinical Pastoral Orientation—an intensive four week course orienting pastors to spiritual care in a hospital setting. The course was scheduled from 8 a.m.to 5 p.m. Mondays through Fridays for the month of January.

I was delighted when I discovered Darrell would be in the group with me at Bethany Methodist Medical Center in Kansas City, Kansas. The course was designed as a mini-plunge into Clinical Pastoral Education which is the formal training required of hospital chaplains. It was a great program and I learned quite a lot I would put to use in the years to come.

It was at Bethany during my first all night coverage in a hospital where I first worked with a man through the final stages of his wife's death by cancer. It was very emotional, even painful for me, but I felt I had been some help to a man who seemed so broken by his great loss.

I was assigned to visit patients on a certain ward each day and became friends with one older lady who was there for a couple of weeks. One day I noticed a change in her. Her daughter said they had changed some of her medication and she was doing better. After a few minutes of conversation she asked me what had happened to my eye. She was referring to my birthmark. It is a hemangioma covering my right eyelid, brow and an inch or so of my forehead. The old medical term is port wine stain.

121

I told her it was just my birthmark and she argued it had not been there on any of our previous visits. It was obvious she was embarrassed she had mentioned it at all. She was soon weeping her apologies and no amount of words from me or her daughter could assuage her pain and tears.

Part of the CPO program was to learn to write ministry action reports. I wrote up the encounter with the patient as a verbatim report and presented it to my peer group and supervisor. It had upset me that my birthmark had been a source of emotional pain and embarrassment for this wonderful lady. As we discussed the encounter someone asked if I had ever considered having it removed.

My honest answer was, "Not much until now." This incident had me thinking about it. My birthmark had been changing some, getting thicker and growing some nodules called blebs, which tended to bleed easily if bumped. My supervisor mentioned there had been some medical breakthroughs using laser light on birthmarks. It was something to consider.

During the January term I got serious about working on my weight and physical conditioning. Since the second fall term I had been assigned a roommate named Pat who commuted from Ames, Iowa. Pat and I had been faithful to jog every day after classes.

He was not there for the January term and it was bitterly cold outside. I had to find some cardio activity to help me lose weight so I ran in the stairwell in the dormitory twice a day. I ran up and down two flights of stairs and kept track of laps by my 60 memorized verses. It worked again and I began to lose weight.

At the end of the January CPO course my supervisor told me I had done well and would likely benefit from additional CPE. I really wanted to try it but could not see my way clear to add CPE to my accelerated schedule to graduate. Kathy was carrying more than her share of the family load and I needed to finish as soon as possible.

My Air Force commissioning physical was scheduled for the end of February. When Pat returned for the spring terms it was easier to bundle up and brave the cold Kansas City winds on our afternoon runs. I still kept up my early morning workout in the stairwell. I had been working on my diet basically by portion control.

Even with all of this effort it still looked close on my weight as I approached the day of my physical at the Kansas City Military Entrance Processing Station. I didn't eat anything in the final 24 hours. I passed with pounds to spare and celebrated with a McDonald's double cheeseburger on the way back to campus. It tasted great.

When the commissioning paperwork arrived in early March a fellow student swore me into the Air Force Reserve as a Chaplain Candidate, Second Lieutenant. He was an Army Chaplain Candidate, Second Lieutenant himself. It was pretty exciting for us both.

There was a family event this winter that demonstrates the missionary heart of the West family. We were very busy and nearing the knot at the end of our rope. Kathy was working her job as the business manager at Midwest Lincoln-Mercury in Joplin and taking care of everything to do with our home and children in her normal fine fashion. We were also very busy at church—me with music and her with Girls In Action.

Needless to say, by Sunday afternoons we were exhausted. This one particular Sunday had been heartrending and informative for our middle child Elizabeth. We called her Beth back then. Either in Sunday School or in the worship service, she had heard God's call to do something for the poor in the Joplin area.

In the lull between Sunday activities Kathy and I sat down at home. Of course we fell asleep as soon as we did. We awakened from our Sunday afternoon nap just in time to see Beth and her four year old brother Billy pulling a wagon up the gravel driveway. When they got closer we realized it was full of groceries—canned goods, hamburger helper, cereal, and such. They both looked very pleased. Of course we asked them where they had come from and the whole story spilled out.

Convicted by the Holy Spirit and convinced that she should do something for the poor, Beth had enlisted her cute little brother in a wonderful scheme. She made a sign that read, "Food for the poor, please donate." That's all it said. They pulled the wagon along the street and while Beth waited at the curb with the wagon she would send Billy up to ring the doorbell and display his sign to the neighbors. The neighbors were moved with compassion or something because the wagon was full when they returned home.

Beth and Billy were very pleased that they were serving God and it showed on their faces. Kathy and I looked at each other in horror knowing that our neighbors thought the West's had sent our children out door-to-door begging for food—for us! Ahgh! Elizabeth and Billy gave their gifts to the local rescue mission.

Before the end of the first eight week spring term I had been asked by Pastor Phillip McClendon to serve as Interim Minister of Youth at Calvary Baptist Church in Joplin. We had joined this church as soon as we moved back to the Joplin area. It was a great church and they would pay me a couple of hundred dollars a week so it was easy to say yes but not so easy to make the extra trips back for Wednesday night activities.

It required a lot of travel but I did get to see a little more of my family. I inherited a huge concert project from the previous youth minister. He had contracted with contemporary Christian singing artist Russ Taff for a Thursday night concert in our 2000 seat auditorium. The old youth minister still lived in the area and did most of the work. It was a great concert and I was very impressed with Russ Taff's character and talent, especially when we came up a few hundred dollars short of our contracted fee. He just praised God and hugged our necks.

Billy made an early Friday morning trip back to Kansas City with me. What a great experience for me to have my son hang out with me at school. One interesting twist to this trip was when Billy met my roommate, Pat, it was obvious he did not like him. Billy wasn't rude or anything but did not respond to this warm and outgoing man like most people did.

As the school year progressed Pat and I continued to run together daily. Before the end of the spring terms we actually jogged ten miles one afternoon. It was quite an accomplishment for me. Pat shared with me how he was praying about leaving his Baptist Student Union work at Iowa State and starting an intentional corporate disciple-making ministry in Des Moines. I encouraged him and prayed for him. The closer we got to the end of the school year the more distant Pat became to me. It was puzzling.

Sometime during the spring our landlord in Carl Junction told us he was planning to sell his house. Kathy and I started praying and looking for something which would allow us to keep the kids in the Carl

Junction school district. We were driving around one Sunday afternoon and noticed an empty house on a corner lot in the Lone Elm Subdivision.

The yard was a mess. Trash had been burned and left in the front yard and the septic tank was uncovered in the back yard. When we looked in the windows of what appeared to be a three- bedroom ranch style house with one bathroom. We could see many holes in the walls. It looked like a lot of punching and kicking had been going on.

By the time of my midweek call to Kathy she had found the bank which owned the house and was starting the necessary processes for us to buy it for $27,000. The father of two young people in the youth group sent his sheet rock crew from his remodeling and construction business to repair the walls free of charge. We were ready to move in just as I was finishing finals.

Our friends from Calvary helped us get moved just in time for me to leave for my first summer chaplain candidate assignment. I flew to Montgomery, Alabama, to attend the two-week Chaplain Candidate Orientation Course at the Chaplain School of the Air University housed on Maxwell Air Force Base. There were 85 of us from all over the country and from many different faith groups. I enjoyed the experience but missed Kathy and the kids.

Following graduation we were given orders to travel directly by air to our 49 day summer assignments. No one was allowed to go home enroot. My assignment was Altus AFB near Altus, Oklahoma. I had never heard of it before. It was way out in western Oklahoma.

I was welcomed on arrival and put to work immediately. It was a great assignment where I was allowed to use my gifts and talents as I learned about Air Force chaplaincy first hand. I lived in the BOQ (Bachelor Officer Quarters) and rented a motor scooter from Recreation Supply for transportation.

Kathy and the kids came out to spend the second weekend with me. Kathy was exhausted from the ten hour drive. We were allowed to stay in brand new temporary family quarters for the weekend. I had missed them so much. It was really great. The kids were excited to see me and tell me about the trip. As one they told me about seeing some mountains in the distance and being surprised and disappointed when they got closer to discover they were—just a pile of rocks—which is a very accurate description of the strangely beautiful Wichita Mountains.

The Altus assignment was a great experience for me. The chaplains and chapel staff were wonderful and worked hard to get me a wide variety of Air Force chaplain experiences. I led the choir and small worship orchestra. I also preached several times in Chapel services and was sent to fill the pulpit one Sunday for the Presbyterian Church at Mangum, Oklahoma. Mangum is famous for an annual rattlesnake festival. I remembered an old Windy Bagwell gospel ballad about handling serpents and was pleased to be preaching in the Presbyterian Church and not the Pentecostal Church of Mangum.

One of my assignments was to visit patients in the base hospital. It was interesting and enjoyable work. My first memorial service for a young family whose baby died shortly after birth was sad. There were also fun things. I made two long ministry-of-presence flights with C-141 Starlifter and KC-135 Stratotanker crews. The Starlifter flight featured an in-flight emergency landing at Charleston Air Force Base. What a blessing. I was able to visit and have lunch with my old friend Chaplain Wally Hucabee from Shemya days who was serving as the Senior Protestant Chaplain there.

In my spare time I jogged, worked out at the base gym, and took up ceramics again. I poured, cleaned, and fired a large nativity set at the base hobby shop. Amy, Elizabeth, and Billy would help me stain them if I could get them home in good shape. The chapel pianist was Cathy MacDonald. She and her family were always good to have me over for dinner or take me water skiing and tubing at Lake Altus.

The summer was long but the second lieutenant pay was a much appreciated addition to our finances. By the time the summer was over I was more than ready to get home. I could tell in my phone conversations with the kids they were getting excited about me coming home too. I knew Kathy was ready for some help even though it would be limited with school starting soon. Each of the children told me they had a special birthday surprise for me when I got home. I'll get to that in a while.

As the day to fly home approached, my emotions became troubled. I was glad to be going home but sad about leaving my new friends. The emotional conflict got me down and I didn't feel well physically. I was invited by the MacDonald's for one more trip to the lake.

I enjoyed riding in the boat but declined my turn to ski. I was, however, willing to ride the tube and soon found myself being dragged along the surface of the lake at 40 miles per hour. I was immediately uneasy. Captain MacDonald had bragged and proved he could flip me over any time he wanted. Actually, flying through the air, flopping into the water and bobbing to the surface had been a lot of fun on previous outings. A high-density foam ski vest can make you amazingly brave. I had loved this before. I was very tense—if not afraid—this time. What was the difference?

The truth and full blown fear hit me like a ton of bricks—I was not wearing a life jacket! It took all my strength to hang on to the tube handle so I could not release one had to signal to stop. I was not too proud to yell but the noise of the boat made it a moot point. After fifteen minutes (seemed like forever) Kathy realized my predicament and had her husband ease the boat down. I was shaken but relieved.

What a difference a life vest makes. I had been fearless before; not caring about being tossed. The life vest would pull me to the surface—I was certain. I may not be the brightest candle in the box but by the time we had the ski boat back on the trailer I understood God was teaching me something besides water safety.

Jesus is my life vest. With the Lord in the center of my life I will always pop to the top no matter where life tosses me. Without trusting in Him, life is like a wild tube ride with no with no safety vest and no certainty for your future. Fear is the way of life without Christ.

The lesson was put to the test the very next morning. The first leg of my journey home was in a four-seat commuter plane from Altus to Oklahoma City. The pilot had me sit in the copilot seat. There was a young couple riding in the rear seats. The pilot chatted with us all while he was making his pre-flight checks. It was still dark out but very warm. The pilot opened his window a little. The curved bubble window was hinged at the top center of the fuselage.

We taxied to the runway and he quickly received clearance to take off in the pre-dawn darkness. As we gathered speed I heard wind whistling somewhere. The pilot said with panic in his voice, "What's that sound?" I immediately remembered he had not latched his window and shouted so. At the instant he grasped the latch with his right hand the window popped up taking his arm with it.

He was, of course, attached to his arm and his body was jerked to the left as he tried to hang on to the window. As he was fighting the window his left-handed grip on the yoke was greatly altered. We swerved back and forth on the runway until he was able to pull the window back into place and idle down the engine. The pilot was embarrassed. After the initial shock wore off I realized how good it was to be wearing my life vest—Jesus.

The rest of the trip home was uneventful. My Kathy and the kids met me at the Joplin airport. After hugs and kisses all around the kids were in a hurry to get me home to my surprise. My birthday had been earlier in the week and I was delighted to receive a new hard case for my archery equipment. But the bow case was not my surprise.

Sometime before leaving for the summer I had spoken with Kathy and stated—in no uncertain terms, "I never wanted another cat in our house." My surprise was great all right—each of the children had their own kitten. I was aware of this before they told me because I could smell where the kittens had been urinating on the threshold of the front door.

What should have been a joyous reunion and birthday celebration was not. I was very angry. Kathy had totally gone against my wishes. I tried to shield the children from my anger but they knew I was not pleased with their surprise. When I asked Kathy why she simply said, "You weren't here and they wanted kittens so badly I couldn't say 'no' to them."

Back on campus I looked up my friend Darrell. His summer had been eventful too. His mother had died and his younger brother, Kevin, was now living with them. The church basement green Ford had been replaced by new GMC S-15. We picked up where we had left off in May.

News about my old roommate hit campus with the returning students. It was reported that he had left the ministry to pursue his relationship with another man in Des Moines. I was shaken but somehow not surprised. I tried to reach him but was only able to speak with a minister in his church. The rumor was true.

Things had gotten even better at Alta Vista. A member of the church had provided Darrell with a silver whale type trailer for him and his family to stay in on the weekends. The folks who owned the land we liked to hunt allowed them to place the trailer there. It was great! I don't know what Janice thought about it but we saw its great potential for a hunting camp.

In our pre-season scouting I had found a likely place in a draw between two milo fields. Once again, the best possible perch was a locust tree—covered with those long nasty thorns. Remembering how the hard work had paid off last year, I gladly pruned and prepared the tree for my stand.

I saw several deer from this stand during the early part of bow season but they never came close enough. One afternoon the week before gun season opened Darrell and I managed to make our way to Alta Vista for an afternoon hunt. The first thing we did was relocate Darrell's lean-up ladder stand to the western, upper edge of the draw I would be hunting. Due to a huge population of bois d'arc trees Darrell had named it Hedgeball Holler. The farmer had begun harvesting the milo in the Darrell's field in large round bales but his equipment had broken after two trips around. We were both excited because there was plenty of rutting sign everywhere. The only problem was it was unseasonably warm.

My stand had me facing up the holler. As sundown approached I was shocked to catch movement at the head of the draw. I nearly passed out when I realized I was looking at five bucks—four of which were magnificent. As they came on I lost my mind again. They began to mill around and feed just out of range or in places I had not prepared shooting lanes. I didn't let it stop me and quickly emptied my quiver and watched as all six arrows bounced around what I should have named Pinball Holler.

With my last futile attempt the biggest of the bunch cut out and left the holler headed Darrell's way. Within a minute I heard Darrell's whistle. When I climbed down and began to retrieve my arrows the herd of deer just stood there and watched me. It was obvious they had nothing to fear from me.

When I reached Darrell's location he was looking at the ground in the edge of the uncut milo. He told me he had hit the deer, probably a little back. It had hunched up and then took off and left the field at a very steep spot. It was almost dark by then but Darrell could see the doubt on my face. It had been a long shot. "Forty steps," Darrell said.

He was bothered by my lack of faith in his marksmanship and quickly dumped out his plastic spit cup and placed it upside-down on a cut milo stalk about eighteen inches high. He climbed back up on his stand and promptly drilled the cup with an arrow. He made a believer out of me.

We found one drop of blood where the buck had bailed off the hill-top field. It did not look good. It was dark in color which fit with Darrell's judgment his arrow had struck the deer too far back for a quick, clean kill. With full dark approaching we opted to spend the night at the trailer. We would have to cut classes the next day but it would have been unethical to abandon the wounded deer. I had brought study material and we settled in for the long night. I awakened several times during the night and heard coyotes howling. I'm not sure Darrell slept at all.

Since I was there, I hunted my Hedgeball Holler stand early the next morning. No deer were moving around me. I do remember seeing a shooting star on the eastern horizon. I also saw a coyote slip across the draw and heard the squeal when he caught his breakfast rabbit.

When I found Darrell, he was hung up on the same spot of blood trail we had found the night before. We saw scuff marks where the buck had touched down a couple of times descending the steep slope but nothing else at the bottom. The bottom was a short but steep sided draw which met Hedgeball Holler on the right side. I wanted to go down the draw but Darrell said he felt certain the deer went up the draw toward the thick woods where I had taken my buck last year. We looked for a couple of hours and found nothing.

We quit for a while and found something to eat. I settled in back at the trailer to study and Darrell went to borrow the landowners four-wheeled all-terrain vehicle. It was the first one of those I had ever seen. After studying for over an hour something caught my attention. When

I looked out the open trailer door I saw Darrell waving from the next hilltop.

I made my way to him, ready to hear the story he was obviously anxious to tell. He said he had found himself once again at the bottom of the slope where we lost the trail—frustrated and desperate. He prayed for God to help him find the deer. He looked down and saw a light colored rock with a dark brown spot on it. He picked it up and deposited some spit (he was good at that) next to the spot. When he worked the spittle over the spot it turned red. He stuck a small stick into the ground where he had picked up the rock.

Darrell moved slowly down the draw (like I had originally suggested) and within 15 feet found another dried drop of blood. The pattern continued for maybe 50 yards and he decided to push forward on the line. When he came to the three-strand fence at the end of the draw he found blood on one of the wires. He looked up and saw his buck laying not far beyond the fence. He was very glad and so was I.

Possums or some such critters had dined on the fellow's innards overnight, but other than that and the fact he had been laying out in 80 degree weather, it was just fine. We hated to lose the meat but were very glad to find the 8-pointer. Darrell had it scored and mounted.

It qualified for the Missouri Big Bucks Club book for North of the Missouri River. It was a huge deer with a very hefty rack.

I did not take a deer in 1987 but there is one memorable event I want to share. Since we had been seeing so many bucks at Alta Vista, Darrell invited me to hunt opening day of gun season with him. Daylight opening morning found me seated on a stump down-slope from the northern end of the biggest milo field. I could see the north fence line. The fence was overgrown with vines and brush. A winter wheat field was adjacent on the left. Straight ahead of me was a hay field. At the far end of the field—probably 400 yards—was a farm house, complete with barns, outbuildings, and old rusty vehicles.

It was very cold. Legal hunting light was actual sunrise. I was alert and watchful. Suddenly a shot rang out—very close. As I immediately rotated my wrist to check my watch there was a definite thump in the ground eight to ten feet to my left. My head snapped that direction just in time to see the leaves settling back to earth.

My first thoughts were fearful but quickly translated to anger. I thought perhaps someone was messing with me. I was within 40 yards of the property line. I was wearing all the required orange and I had permission to be where I was. I stubbornly jumped up on the stump to make myself more visible, and maybe a better target—not the brightest thing I have ever done.

I was boiling inside as I looked for the culprit. Within minutes I saw orange-cloaked movement coming from the distant farmhouse. It was a man and a boy. They came in on a straight line toward my position. They stopped on the other side of the fence and began casting about for sign. They followed a trail into the winter wheat field and soon gave up the search. They never looked up my way and did not see me. I considered saying something to them but I held my voice and position.

The morning hunt was pretty well over for me. As the man and boy made their way back to the farmhouse I thought about what had just happened. Here's my theory. There must have been a deer or coyote on the other side of the fence. It was screened from my sight by the vegetation. The man or boy (probably the man) took a shot at the animal and made an elevation adjustment because of the long distance. I have noticed over the years when hunters (including me) hold high on a shot they overcompensate. It seemed to be the case here.

My anger at the incident was hot but before I met up with Darrell, Philip, and Kevin my thoughts had turned. I had taken shots before with a wooded background, assuming because I could not see orange, the woods were empty of hunters. I did not like what had happened to me but it could have been much worse. The shooter had made a big, near disastrous assumption. I realized God had protected me and others from several such assumptions in my past. My thoughts turned to gratitude toward God and grace toward the shooter. I determined to be more careful of my shot selection in the future.

We all went to a local café for breakfast. No one there was friendly to us. Since we were not locals, we were considered to be stupid hunters from the city. Darrell grinned and spoke with a low voice, "Do you think one of these nice guys took a shot at you?"

Chapter 17

1988: A Year of Hard Lessons

January of 1988 found me on a break from school but hard at work for Calvary Baptist Church as an associate pastor for counseling. This was an unpaid position to meet my ministry setting requirement for Theological Field Education. When classes were in session I would work the weekend through Monday. On term breaks I worked more hours but still had more time for the kids. We went roller skating and rented movies and video games.

January was also the month I reestablished a workout regimen. I was an officer in the Air Force now and needed to be in shape for my upcoming summer tour. Our neighborhood was good for running most days and I would race walk around the large sanctuary at Calvary if the weather was bad.

On a semester break trip home to Springfield my mother mentioned my birthmark looked different. She suggested I see a doctor. A friend recommended a dermatologist in Springfield and I was able to get an appointment. He was a nice man and assured me there was nothing pathological going on with my birthmark. He explained it was natural and expected for hemangiomas to grow thicker and uneven with age. He indicated my only course of action would be laser treatments, which he did not do. When he learned I was spending a lot of time in Kansas City he recommended Kansas University Medical Center in Kansas City, Kansas.

I made an appointment with the dermatology clinic there when classes resumed I and was some nervous as I kept it. Two dermatologists looked at my birthmark and agreed I needed laser treatment, which they did not perform. One of them made a call and soon I was introduced to Dr. K., an ophthalmologist.

He led me to another part of the huge hospital and explained what he proposed to do with a series of experimental yellow dye laser treatments. I agreed and he proceeded to treat a small satellite birthmark high on my forehead. He made an appointment for me to return for a more extensive treatment on a Monday in February.

It was snowing when I awakened in Carl Junction that Monday morning. I considered calling to cancel my appointment but I was both excited and anxious to get on with the process. My 1985 Ford Ranger was already loaded with the week's stuff so I left much earlier than I had planned. I was determined to keep my appointment despite the hazardous weather conditions.

U. S. Highway 71 was in pretty good shape because the Highway Department plow crews were doing their jobs well, I thought. My little pickup had decorative running boards which were soon loaded heavy with slush and ice. This actually helped with stability and control. I was able to drive 45 miles per hour with no problems, I thought.

Just north of Nevada, Missouri, I found myself tail-end-Charlie of a long, slow line of assorted vehicles in the right hand lane. I eased out into the left lane and began passing them all. At the head of this caravan was a mail carrier pulling two long trailers. Just as I was pushing through the blinding swirl whipped up by the tractor, I was startled to see the snowplow had turned left on a U-turn lane and deposited a huge pile of snow, blocking my lane ahead.

There was not much time to think and only a few hundred yards to travel. To use the brakes in these conditions was out of the question. If I tried to break through the pile, could I maintain enough control to avoid the oversized rig to my right? I decided not and gently accelerated. I was able to move over in front of the tractor with no room to spare but the move itself broke my traction. My pickup fishtailed to the right—I corrected to the left. Normally I could control a skid by not over controlling but the combination of slick, speed and weight trumped my overblown skills.

After the second slide to the right I knew I was losing it. I certainly did not want to spin 360 with the mail man on my tail. When I corrected back to the left I requested heavenly help and let the Ranger run for the snow covered median. When I entered the median I cut the wheels hard to the left and spun to a stop. The engine died. I watched the vehicles I had just passed pass me by. I'm sure there was plenty of head shaking and grumbling going on in those safely moving vehicles.

I discovered the reason my engine had died—I had not disengaged the clutch. My cry for help had been heard. It was instinctive for me to depress the clutch pedal in such situations but not doing so had caused the engine to stop me sooner than brakes could have.

The four cylinder engine started easily and I pulled back onto the highway. With my mission before me, I pressed on. I slowly picked up speed and quickly gained on the slow moving caravan and slipped past it with ease. I am sure cussing was added to the head shaking this time. I was an idiot.

When I reached my 45 mph cruising speed there was considerable vibration in the front end of my truck. I took the Rich Hill exit, which was my normal break stop, and checked out my vehicle. The white spoke wheels were packed with snow and I quickly cleared it with a snow brush then hit the road once again. The caravan had passed me during the pit stop. I smiled and waved as I passed them for the third time. I was surely an idiot.

Surprisingly, I made it safely to the medical center and received my laser treatment. I went to Darrell's when I arrived on the seminary campus. It was still snowing and the Kansas City area schools were closed. Darrell loved cold, wintry weather and we played outside with the kids. I spent the night on their couch and suffered nightmares all night long of crash after crash into various immovable objects. When I awakened the next morning I admitted to myself I had been an idiot. I also discovered my right eye was swollen shut so I was glad when seminary classes were cancelled for the first time in school history.

On my trip home at the end of the week I found where I had entered the median. That particular section of median was the shallowest and smoothest in the entire stretch of highway. I thanked God again and vowed not to be so stubborn and stupid.

Early in the term I discovered word processing. Up until then I had been satisfied with an electric typewriter with four lines of memory. One of the students rooming near me in the basement of the student dormitory brought an Amstrad word processor to school. He was a commuter like me. I saw what the green screen monster could do and I was ready to step up but couldn't afford the move.

The Amstrad had been marketed by Sears and was already being left behind by the personal computer. Sears was still selling them for around $400. The word processor utilized a 3" floppy disc, which confused me because there was nothing floppy about it. It also featured a byte or two of machine drive allowing you to copy a file to a separate floppy disc. The price seemed impossible.

There was a Venture store across the street from the seminary campus. One day while passing through the electronics department I discovered an Amstrad word processor, complete with screen, key board, and dot matrix printer. Someone had stolen the software. The price was $65.

I hustled back to the dorm and asked the student with the Amstrad if I could use his software to boot up if I bought one. Since the product had run its course and was swiftly disappearing, the software was not readily available to purchase. My friend agreed and so did Kathy when I called her. I made the seemingly grand leap from typing to word processing and wondered how I had survived so many years as a student without one.

My spring classes were critical as I began my run for the prize— graduation in May. The most interesting of my final classes was a one-hour course called Credo. There was only one assignment: prepare a paper (minimum 30 pages) on our personal theology and trace the influences and seeds of thought through our life and education. It was tough to get started but eventually the paper began to flow and grow. I really enjoyed the project and was pleased with the final product and my grade.

Kathy and I are not 100% sure about when but we think it was during this term when Billy scared us to death. Actually Kathy had the biggest scare because she was there. I was 200 miles away at school. Her memory is sketchy about this incident but she remembers seeing Billy coming across the yard toward the house limping and hobbling, in obvious pain. It broke her heart. When she discovered his legs were swollen and blotchy with what looked like blood blisters she took him to the hospital immediately. On the hospital parking lot she locked the keys in her car with the engine running, which is a good indicator of how upset she was. The dealership where she worked brought her another key.

The diagnosis was Henoch-Schoenlein purpura. We monitored Billy's health with daily observation for ketones, doctor's appointments, and lab tests for months. There was some question about his kidney function. Billy was scared by all of this. When the seriousness of the situation finally became clear to me, I was too. Billy got better, thank God, even though we still had unanswered questions.

Darrell and his family had discovered bleacher seat tickets for Royals games were only $5.00. As the weather warmed we took in several games. We preferred the left field bleachers so we could watch Bo Jackson play ball and add hulls to a huge pile of sunflower debris he was amassing on the warning track. To keep from feeling too guilty for playing while at school and to prepare for finals I always brought my note cards and drilled church history facts between innings.

Time for my graduation was at hand. I was excited about graduation as I wore my class A blue uniform to a pre-graduation banquet with classmates and professors. I watched a group of Doctor of Ministry candidates perform a funny skit and wondered if that degree could possibly be in my future.

Kathy brought the kids to Kansas City the day before graduation. Her parents joined us there as well. I skipped a reception at the seminary president's residence and went to a Royals vs. Rangers baseball game with the whole gang.

It was a fun vacation for us. My parents and grandmother also attended the graduation ceremony as I graduated with Honors (2 thousandths of a GPA point from Highest Honors) and received the Baptist Bookstore Award for Excellence in the Study and Practice of Preaching. It was a surprising and pleasing recognition. Many of the preacher students were shocked because I was better known on campus as a singer.

My buddy Darrell, who would graduate the next year, was an usher at my ceremony. He had been in my preaching classes and later told me he was not surprised with the award because he had seen my work and had heard something from one of the professors in the days leading up to graduation.

After the event and pictures we spent the rest of the day and evening at Worlds of Fun—a great Kansas City theme park. We had a wonderful time. Even at the close of this long dreamed of and waited for day I could feel the old creep of uncertainty, fear, and depression stirring in the back of my heart.

But that pity party would have to wait. I was ordained to the gospel ministry by Calvary Baptist Church and by mid-June was off to my second and final Air Force chaplain candidate assignment. The location was much closer this time—Whiteman AFB at Knobnoster, Missouri. Whiteman's main mission involved hundreds of nuclear missiles scattered around central Missouri. It was a good assignment in some respects and I learned many things about a different part of the Air Force.

I was initially disappointed because I did not experience the freedom and support I had at Altus AFB. My first day on the job I was introduced to a junior chaplain, a captain, who immediately had me running errands for him. Those chores included picking up his laundry at the downtown drycleaners. He acted like he was a general and I was his dog robber (Aid de Camp).

I really did like the assignment and most of the people but the base was kind of ugly. When the senior chaplain got wind of my dog-robbing duties they stopped. The senior chaplain also taught me a couple of great lessons. One day he called me into his office for a progress report. He was impressed I was using a word processor to keep a detailed log of my work. At one point in our conversation he pointed to the silver oak leafs on his dark blue epaulets and said, "This is my pay grade." He pointed to the blue and silver cross pinned over his left breast pocket and said, "This is my calling. This is why I am here. You will do well as a chaplain if you keep that in mind."

Another lesson from this wonderful chaplain was brevity. He was famous and highly sought after for his short invocation prayers. His most famous prayer was delivered at a Dining In. A Dining In is a formal military dinner event requiring Mess Dress uniform (a beautiful tuxedo type uniform) for all attendees. When called upon to pray he stood at the podium and said, "Lord, bless this Mess. Amen." Then he sat down.

The youth leader for the protestant chapel program was an instructor pilot for the Air Rescue and Recovery Squadron housed at Whiteman. This was the only flying mission on the base at the time. They flew a late model of the UH1—Huey—helicopter.

One day I got a call from him and he asked if I was up for going along on a night check flight. I had wanted to ride on a Huey since my early firefighter days at Fairchild AFB and couldn't contain my excitement as I answered affirmatively. He took care of the paperwork and I reported to the flightline for pre-flight briefing at dusk of the appointed day. I was not the only extra passenger. The Flight Surgeon was going along to log his required flying hours.

It was clear and warm as we took off with the doors locked back. I was strapped into the seat by the left rear door. I'm sure I had a silly grin on my face for the entire flight. We headed west toward Kansas City as the last of the sun was slipping over the horizon. The Royals were playing that night and we made several orbits of the stadium on our way in. I have lost the pictures from the rare perspective of the game I snapped with a 110 camera—high tech of those days.

We made practice approaches to several hospitals in the Kansas City metroplex. I had often seen the huge red balls attached to power lines but until I was on an aircraft flying among them I had no idea what they were for. As we passed close by them on every downtown landing I was glad they had a purposeful function. They helped the pilot steer clear of the dangerous power line hazards.

We orbited the game a few more times on our way outbound. As we flew eastward over the seemingly endless, rolling wheat fields of central Missouri the moon rose high and bright. I will never forget seeing the amazing moon shadow silhouette of the Huey on the on the golden grain fields. It reminded me of a scorpion. We made landings at a couple of missile launch control facilities. The flight ended way too soon for me.

My candidate tour ended on a Monday. I reported to Mt. Vernon, Missouri, and met our church's children's camp contingency at Baptist Hill. Kathy was leading this group and had enlisted me to be a counselor for a cabin of boys who were enrolled to take the Missouri Hunter Education course during the week. It was really good to see Kathy and the kids. Amy and Beth were campers. Billy was too young to be a camper but he stayed in the cabin with me. It was really a great time.

Billy could read some even though he had not started school yet. His sister, Elizabeth, had been teaching him to read. She was destined to be a teacher. He and I studied together as we attended the hunter education class with my group every afternoon. We passed the course and he even made a better score than I did. He was pretty proud of that. So was I.

Back during my summer assignment I had traveled to Kansas City for a laser treatment and had stopped to shop at U. S. Toys and Creative Playthings. I had bought enough trinkets and junk for my cabin full of boys to have something special each day of camp.

The first day of camp I gave them Panama straw hats. It really helped me keep a running count of my very active boys. On succeeding days I gave the boys fake teeth, Groucho Marx type glasses, nose and mustache, pirate eye patches, and such. It was great fun except some of the other counselors complained.

After camp we all headed home. It was good to be home but I did not have a job. The Air Force was in a reduction mode and my endorsing agency, the Home Mission Board of the Southern Baptist Convention, required two years of pastoral experience after graduation before they would even think about recommending one of their chaplains for active duty. My dream of being an active duty Air Force chaplain would have to wait.

Back during the school year my pastor, Phillip McClendon, had talked about a staff job after graduation but I had pretty much blown it by speaking too frankly and, from my perspective, honestly to one of his staff ministers about her personality issues. I allowed myself to get verbally backed into a corner and was too stubborn to just shut up and walk away. My unwise comments had brought me unofficially into persona non grata status.

I loved working with Phillip and was often amazed at how God blessed him as he led the largest Baptist church in the four-state region. We did not always agree and often failed at communication but I loved him and still do. He was a great pastor to learn from.

We were still active in the church and loved it. One day I found the courage to ask Phillip if there was any possibility of a job at Calvary. He told me the maintenance man was behind and I could work temporarily helping him catch up. It wasn't what I was hoping for but I swallowed my pride and accepted the opportunity. I knew what needed to be done and fell to the nastiest tasks with a humble vengeance. The carpet in the pre-school area was crusted with dried playdough. The custodian would not touch the job so I spent several days on my knees freezing the stuff with cans of spray Freon and breaking the junk loose from the carpet fibers with a large spoon. The room looked great when I was finished.

While on this project several staff members had stopped by to chat. Our young youth minister was obviously bothered when he saw me down scraping the floor. God had allowed me to help him keep his job when the pastor wanted to fire him earlier in the year. He was visibly upset and said as much. He wanted to go speak to Phillip on my behalf. I encouraged him to be faithful to his calling and not worry about me. God would "lift me up in due time." (1 Peter 5:6) In my heart I knew this was the only job I deserved at the time. I had put Phillip in a tough spot with my mouth.

Before I finished the project the pastor came by to see me. He too was visibly shaken when he saw me working on the floor. He asked me to come by his office and talk about an associate pastor position he had in mind for me. God was—and is—good to me.

Our lives settled down to something very busy but normal. I was home every evening at some point. Life was moving very swiftly for us. One incident underscores how busy we were. During this time Kathy was digging out from under an employee embezzlement situation at her work. My responsibilities always involved several programs and events. We were both so busy and overwhelmed each of us assumed the other would deposit their paychecks in the bank.

We once again proved the axiom it is never safe to assume anything. We did not discover this until our banking institution informed us our financial outlook was vulcanized. Five checks bounced and the fees didn't add up, they multiplied. We both felt pretty foolish. Thankfully, one of our deacons in the church was a vice-president at our savings and loan and managed to bail us out with only one fee to pay. We never let that happen again.

October found the Would-be Woodsman bow hunting on the

Lohman Call Company lease in the Fort Crowder industrial zone. My friend, Brad Harris, was the professional hunter for the company. I had met him while on staff at First Baptist Church in Neosho. He allowed me to archery hunt a remote portion of their leased land which was inside the corporate boundaries of Neosho.

I hunted a few evenings from a portable stand overlooking an old tractor trail on a transition line between dense brush and a stand of hardwoods. On one particular evening I discovered a ground scrape had been opened in the edge of the trail below my perch. It was very windy and my sense of hearing was lost in the wind. After a brief look to the rear of my position I was startled to find a doe had entered the scrape while my head was turned. I quietly drew my bow, holding my top sight pin on her right front side.

While holding, my mind drifted off into a self-debate on whether I should take this deer or wait for a better one. "The season was young but so were my children." "If I take this doe, I can check harvesting a deer by archery off of my manly to do list for the year." "I could focus more on my family and my ministry." "I pray every day for God's will in my life, this deer might be a part of His plan." I made a good case for shooting the doe and with the decision made, my mind came back to real time and before I was ready the arrow was on the way. The only problem was the doe did not honor my mental time out. She had moved just enough for my premature released arrow to miss her heart and lung area and strike in the spine six inches or so in front of her tail.

The deer dropped on the spot. I was horrified that she was down, hurt, and crawling away using her front legs. My panic at this sight helped the two arrows I launched to finish the job go wide right and wide left. Disgusted with myself, I climbed down the tree and ran to the deer as I was drawing my big Schrade belt knife. She was also terrified. With her rear legs paralyzed I was able to immobilize her front legs and head. I asked her forgiveness as I completed the gory task at hand.

During the firearm deer season I hunted from the same stand with my bow on opening day. I stayed above the ground from before daylight until dark. One eight-point buck passed by out of range. My deer hunting for the year was over.

144

When I called Darrell and told him I had harvested a doe in the early bow season he replied, "Wayne, you are better than that. You should have waited for a buck." My answer was, "I didn't feel better than that." The Would-be Woodsman would have to wait for another year.

It was time to focus on my family. I thanked God for a successful season and lessons learned. The Would-be Woodsman's goal is to always harvest game quickly and humanely. Sometimes it doesn't work out that way and then you've got to be willing to do whatever it takes to finish the job. It was a hard lesson. I had also learned it is not always expedient to speak everything you think. Even if it is true, or you think it is true, it might not be necessary to say it.

Chapter 18

1989: The Cross Pen Buck

When I was commissioned into the Air Force Chaplain Candidate program there was an expectation, if not a promise, of an assignment as a chaplain in an Individual Mobilization Augmentee slot at some active duty airbase. Things had changed since then and there were not enough positions for those of us completing the program in 1988. Someone came up with the plan to extend us as chaplain candidates until things loosened up. The downside was, I would have to remain a second lieutenant for a year longer than usual. Another bum deal was I would have to do drill time for points only—no pay.

The upside was, I was still an Air Force Reserve officer with hopes for a future career and my extension assignment was Whiteman AFB. Another blessing in all of this was the Air Force Reserve required all extended candidates to meet in Denver for an instructional conference. It was a pretty cool (and cold) trip and I made some money and retirement points for the three day conference. I also renewed friendships made at Chaplain Candidate School. It was comforting to know I was not the only one who waited for an assignment and promotion. While regular monthly training time was for retirement points only, they did pay us for a twelve day annual tour. The money really came in handy.

My work at Calvary Baptist Church was very interesting but I was challenged on one particular front. Part of my unofficial function was to troubleshoot organizational and staff problems. I had a friend on staff whose personal choices stirred up concern among other staffers and some church members. I went to him and raised some of those questions to get his view on things. We had what I thought was a pretty good meeting.

The following day I briefed Phillip on the gist of our conversation and didn't think much more about it. That is, until the he called me to his office several days later and wanted me to give him a copy of the list of concerns I had gone over with the staffer. I was reluctant and said so. I was concerned my sincere desire to help a friend and fellow staff member find his way through some controversy and become a better servant would somehow have the opposite effect. Phillip assured me his intentions were similar and I believed him, and still do. However, others became involved and that opposite effect I feared became reality. Within a month my friend was forced to move on. To this day I do not know or understand the details of this nightmare.

Darrell, his brother Kevin, and son Philip came down from Kansas City to fish the March 1st opening day of trout season in the state parks. We stayed at a friend's place near Eagle Rock on Tablerock Lake so we could get to Roaring River State Park before daylight. I have always loved taking skeptics to this amazing event. No one wants to believe me when I describe the scene of thousands of anglers lined elbow to elbow along a narrow stream casting simultaneously when the sunrise horn sounds. I love to see the look on their face when they realize I wasn't even exaggerating about ice forming on the rod tips.

At the end of a busy summer I received good news. The President was appointing me a commission as a Chaplain, First Lieutenant in the United States Air Force Reserve. Several friends at church planned a commissioning event for me on a Sunday after the evening service. Bob Wilke's father-in-law, a retired officer, did me the honors of administering the oath. At the close of the ceremony Bob gave me a very nice silver Cross pen. It was engraved with "Wayne West, SBP." When I asked him what "SBP" stood for he smiled and said, "Southern Baptist Preacher." I was delighted.

The Would-be Woodsman bow hunted on the Lohman lease early in the season. I hung my API stand near the location I had taken the doe from the previous year. The buck sign was heavy in the wooded side of the treeline so I was facing into the woods over a cluster of small rubs.

The date for going off of Daylight Saving Time is a wonderful event for this bowhunter. The earlier sunrise allows the Would-be Woodsman to hunt for a couple of hours before reporting to church. This can only happen for the minister who is not the senior pastor and has taken care of all the preparations for the busy day at church. The pastor or even the music leader cannot take the chance something could happen and keep them from their Sunday responsibilities. I was the number two associate pastor and thought I could manage an early Sunday morning hunt.

I drove our 1988 Plymouth Voyager van to Neosho and parked in my usual spot. I had removed the rear seat for hunting season. Brad Harris had not only been good enough to let me hunt on the Lohman Company lease but had shared with me some of the free products he had received from other outdoor equipment companies. I applied a doe-in-heat smelling wax stick to trees and limbs on my way in to my stand an hour before daylight.

I witnessed a strange thing in the pre-dawn darkness. Two skunks made their way along the edge of the woods near my stand. One of them was the standard black with white stripe variety but the other was white with a black stripe. I was glad to be up in a tree so I could observe without disturbing them.

Just as it was beginning to get light I put another Brad Harris freebie in play. It was a camouflaged head net. I noticed two does approaching from my far right and then sensed movement to my left. A yearling buck was working the scent trail I had made. When we came beneath my stand I noticed the hairs along the ridge of his back were standing straight up. He seemed really fired up. The chase was on when he saw the two does. They were not too interested in him but the fact didn't stop him from chasing them around the woodlot for half an hour. I really enjoyed the show and eventually tried several calls from my new grunt tube to see what would happen. I did not have the heart to tell the young buck it was not these ladies who had gotten him fired up.

I was so focused on the activity in front of me I did not see the deer slipping in from my left until it was nearly too late. He was looking for something, probably the deer he thought was making the grunting sounds. His headgear appeared to be 12 inch spikes. There was a theory going around in those days which held; a deer with long spikes would probably always be a spike and should be harvested to remove them from the gene pool. I was willing to go along with the theory at the time so when he moved behind a tree I drew my bow. When he stepped clear of the tree at 15 yards I released the arrow.

You probably realize by now the Would-be Woodsman loves accessories. I was trying out a new contraption called The String Tracker. It consisted of spool of tooth floss-like string attached to the arrow shaft just back of the broadhead. The idea was the fine string would pay out as the deer ran off and you would simply follow the string to find the deer.

My arrow struck the deer too high and passed through just below the spine. He took off to my right and I thought I was in trouble until he stopped after just thirty yards. He arched his neck and fell over— done. The broadhead had done its job, passing completely through the deer and leaving a double blood trail after slicing through both major arteries running along the spine.

The string tracker had done its job, hanging onto the arrow and leaving a double string trail to the deer. The scent stick had done its job and stirred up some activity in my vicinity. The freebie head net however, left something to be desired. It was very hard to see through in low light and I did not realize the buck was a forked horn and not a spike. I could blame the head net for my poor shot placement but I won't.

When I planned this early Sunday morning hunt I had not considered I would actually harvest a deer. I dragged the deer to the van and loaded it. Taking the deer to church would not be responsible. Someone would surely see it and be offended. The nearby Neosho Fire Station was a game checkpoint so I took care of that chore on my way to Brad Harris' house. It was unusual to catch him at home during deer season but I did. He helped me hang the deer in his storage building. I washed up, changed into my suit and went to church like nothing had happened.

I don't remember where I hunted on opening day of gun season but I think it was on a friend's property north of Springfield. Wherever it was I didn't even see a deer. I listened to various stories of success and failure at church the next day. One lady told me her son, who was in medical school, had hunted unsuccessfully on their farm near Seneca. He had seen a buck several times on the west end of their property but had gone back to school empty handed. She said his family really needed the meat. I volunteered to hunt for the deer and give them the meat if I shot it. She was thrilled and invited me to come out the next day.

Monday was my day off and I found their farm without much trouble. Her husband described their property boundaries and told me where I could park my van. Their western most field was fallow and bordered on the south and east by fairly thick woods. Stillhunting and scouting around their property took most of the morning. I drove along the eastern edge of the fallow field on my way out, scanning the woods as I eased along.

I was startled to discover a seven point buck checking me out from just 30 yards into the woods. I stopped the van and eased the door open and stepped out. Keeping my eyes on the buck I reached for Max's .308. Still focusing on the buck I reached into the pocket of my O. D. green field jacket and selected a cartridge. Without looking, I opened the bolt and tried to ease the round into the chamber, but for some reason it wouldn't fit. I hated to do it but I broke eye contact with the buck and looked down. I was trying to insert my silver Cross pen into the rifle. I had been looking for it for weeks. The buck slipped away as I laughed at myself. I decided to return there the next morning.

I worked many extra hours at the church so taking a couple of hours off Tuesday morning was not a problem. After parking near the north end of the field I circled through the woods to the south then east. On a tractor trail next to a north-south fence I sat down facing north in the middle of the woods and waited for daylight. It was snowing. There was a low mound to my right which in the light of day turned out to be a coyote den.

The snow squall passed on before daylight and the sun rose to a clear blue sky. I was carrying a new accessory with me. Brad Harris had given me a pair of artificial rattling horns. They were kind of clunky and ugly but I thought I would give them a try. My teeth began to chatter as the sunlight pushed the thermal breezes around me. I decided it was time to rattle something besides my teeth.

I had not rattled the plastic horns together for more than ten seconds when the buck I was looking for appeared between two trees about a hundred yards at my 2 o'clock, looking for me. I eased into prone firing position peeking over the coyote den. My first shot was a miss. That rattled me. My second shot was a miss. He was still looking and I thought, "That deer is dumber than me!" I laid my head on my right arm and tried to calm down. My mind was racing. I couldn't remember how many shots I had fired. I opened the action to check for a round in the chamber and went too far, accidently ejecting the third round. I thought again, "That deer is not dumber than me."

I cycled the bolt for the fourth and final time and sucked in a huge lungful of air. As I relaxed to let the air escape I whispered a prayer and settled the front and rear sights on the deer's left shoulder. He was quartering away to my left and I was determined to make my last shot count. The shot crashed loudly in the barren woods and I saw his tail drop as he charged out of sight to my left. He looked like he might be falling, so I hustled to where I thought he had been standing. It was if he had disappeared into thin air—no deer, no hair, no blood, no tracks. The familiar old feeling of panic and disappointment rose into my throat.

The immediate search for sign was futile so I circled to the north and back to the west. When I cut the fence and tractor trail I worked back to the south looking for sign he had crossed the opening without being seen. I didn't think it was likely but my confidence was very low. When I reached the coyote den mound I got back into firing position and recreated the scene in my mind.

I sighted down the barrel of my empty gun and found the two trees where the deer had been standing and made my way toward the spot focusing on a particular limb all the way. As soon as I passed between the two trees I spotted scuffed leaves and blood. I turned to the left and saw the Cross Pen buck lying dead not ten yards away. My first search

151

had led me 30 yards to the east and the deer's brown coat blended well with the fallen leaves.

The landowners were tickled with the meat for their son's family and I was tickled with the cape and seven point rack. I mounted the deer myself and the head, hide, and horns still hang with my other trophies to remind me of milestones gained and Would-be Woodsman lessons learned. The Cross Pen Buck was the first critter I had specifically hunted and taken. This was also the first time I had been able to gather myself after melting down on both the shot and the blood trail. I gladly acknowledge God had something to do with those things. This was also the first time I had shared all the venison with someone who needed it. The Would-be Woodsman felt good about himself as a hunter and as a person.

Chapter 19

1990: Life Action; God Showed Up

This would be my last year to hunt as a resident in Missouri but as we broke out a new calendar I didn't have a clue about that. Our pastor had led us to commit to a total revival event for late winter. Life Action Ministries would come for two weeks with enough people to take over the action of the church—worship, preaching, singing, and bible study for everyone but the babies.

The logistical preparations fell to me since I was the junior associate pastor. Lodging and meals for 30 people were the biggest challenges. Most members of the team were single men and women in their late teens and early twenties. They would stay in homes with willing church members. The team would prepare two meals each day using our fellowship hall. There were several older members who traveled with their families. They would stay in their fifth-wheel campers. These campers, along with a motor home, required adjustments to our water, power, and sewage utilities. I was not sure it was worth all of the effort.

The effect on our church was amazing. The Life Action Team arrived in force and God moved in the lives of His people, me included. We once again discovered the power of God's presence, the power of a clear conscience, the power of humble submission, and the power of immediate obedience to God's Word. Some uneasy issues among the church staff were dealt with and settled, I thought. Troubled marriages were restored. Some people came to Christ for the first time and the revival meetings were extended into a third week.

God was really dealing with me. I discovered early on I did not have a clear conscience and was living with a lurking fear someone might discover I had not always done the right things. I made a list and committed myself to contact some people and ask forgiveness. This list included a former employer, two of my brothers, and a couple old girlfriends. I began working the list down immediately.

It was my habit in those winter days to do my cardio training inside the church building using the basement hallways or the outside aisle of the worship center. Early one morning (05:30) during the revival I was making laps in the worship center and pouring my heart out to God in prayer as I moved. The church was situated on 30 acres just outside of town overlooking beautiful woods and fields. The side walls of the octagonal room were glass. As the day dawned outside I was thrilled to watch a small doe family of deer feed down the hill on the east side of the church. They walked right past the temporary camper complex like it was not even there.

I became very excited about the deer sighting and stopped what I was doing and went up on the roof to watch the deer. While watching the doe family in the dawn light from the roof it dawned on me I had, in mid-thought, abandoned my conversation with God. It seemed the Would–be Woodsman in me trumped all other concerns in my life at that moment. I realized my life was out of balance—leaning toward the woods. Immediately, I re-entered my prayer time and confessed my sin.

As usual, my response to being out of balance was an all-or-nothing lunge in the opposite direction. The next day I boxed up my archery tackle and took it to a pawn shop intending to sell and give the money to the revival team. The pawnbroker laughed at my request as he pointed to a display rack crowded with compound bows and suggested I wait until summer to sell. This slowed me up enough to think things through. Maybe God did not want me to stop hunting. Maybe He just wanted me to establish priorities and work for balance in my life. After some prayer and meditation on the question I decided to hold off on hunting in the fall until I felt peace about going.

But a lot of things happened before time to hunt in the fall. This was an important year for everyone in the family. I went on active duty orders for the month of May to attend the Chaplain Orientation Course at Maxwell AFB in Montgomery, Alabama. This gave me a great opportunity to spend some time with my buddy Darrell and his family.

He was pastoring Smith Lake Baptist Church near Jasper, Alabama. I spent the night with them on the way down and returned to their home each weekend. Darrell had me preach and sing at his church and we went fishing a lot. I loved it. The Chaplain course was excellent and I made some great friends but the highlight of Chaplain Orientation Class 90B was spending time with Darrell.

Another plus of that month was fiscal: first lieutenant pay was more than I made at home. The temporary increase in income was a really good thing because Kathy's dealership was closing its doors and we were going to try to live on my income and God's provision. It was a stressful time for us but life kept on moving and God always provided a way.

Amy had tried out and made the athletic team at Carl Junction Junior High School. The athletic team divided their talents between volleyball and basketball. She also competed and made the basketball cheerleading squad. I was only able to make a couple of the after-school games she cheered at and not many more of her volleyball games.

I did make one out-of-town trip with Amy's volleyball team. I followed their school bus to Nevada, Missouri, and watched my daughter amaze me and many others. She was not one of the best players so she didn't play a lot but her coach knew she could count on Amy to serve well. When the team got into a bind she would substitute Amy in to serve. Her delivery was an old-school underhand serve and it was magical in its consistency and, for some reason, difficult to return. Each time Amy was brought in she scored six to eight points. I was impressed and proud of my girl. I don't remember if we won but I do remember being pleased I had not let my busy life rob me of an opportunity to see my Amy shine.

Elizabeth was a bright and beautiful child who wanted to fit in with the social life of her peers. It was a big problem for her because of a standard I attempted to hold our family to. Back in my youth ministry days I had become concerned and convinced our culture's way of courting is a way of heartbreak—especially for young ladies. I dubbed the accepted process Playing House.

We encourage young people, even very young people, to pair up (go steady), exchange some tokens (rings, bracelets, pins etc.), declare monogamous loyalty, and break up (divorce) when it doesn't feel right anymore. By the time a person is old enough to make wise decisions they are well schooled in the art of Playing House and divorce seems no big deal. American young people may experience the rollercoaster of marriage and divorce so many times it seems normal. Or, they get so deeply involved and in love with someone they can't find their way out of a bad relationship because of perceived or actual pressure to remain loyal and true.

My rule came in several pieces and my honest goal was to spare my children some unnecessary heartaches. Boyfriends and girlfriends were fine but going steady or dating exclusively was off the table. When my children would be old enough and mature enough to go out on dates they would be strongly encouraged to alternate outing partners, if possible. In other words, they should be open to more than one friend of the opposite sex at a time.

Billy was young enough he didn't care. The girls' biggest argument was boys would say awful things about them. My answer was for them to tell me what was said by whom and I would meet with them and their parents to discuss it. They really didn't like that possibility.

One day I happened to be at home when the kids got off the school bus in front of our house. I went to the door to meet and greet them. Elizabeth was crying. The situation came clear to me in a flash of discernment. Beth had experimented outside my loving bounds. I tried to put my arm around her and ask without too much sarcasm, "Did your boyfriend break up with you?" With a tearful and terrified look she replied, "How did you know?" I didn't have an answer but I went to her room and tried to explain the purpose of my plan was to protect her from such unnecessary and painful heartbreaks. There would be enough of those in life without looking for more. She had learned a great lesson. No further discipline was required.

Billy was eight years old and in the second grade. He played soccer that fall in the Carl Junction parks program. I had never played the game. I had watched Amy play as a young girl in Neosho and my impression of youth soccer brought to mind a school of baby catfish swarming around some tasty morsel. It was boring to me.

The last game of his season would have been a great time to be in the woods. It was a beautiful, clear-skied, and cool October Saturday and I was torn between my desire to hunt and my desire to support my son. My peace meter settled on soccer and I prepared myself for another boring game.

Was I surprised when Billy put on his most outstanding athletic performance, ever? His team was in last place and was matched against the team in next-to-last place which just happened to have Billy's best friend, Ryan Sheffield, as their best player. It must have been the friendly competition that lit Billy's fire. Whatever it was, he was transformed from an uninspired player on a pretty sorry team to an aggressive and confident team leader in search of a championship. He scored four goals in the game and led his team to victory. But there is more to the story.

The win left both teams tied for last and a five man shootout would determine fourth and fifth place. Billy was selected as the goalie for the shootout and it was a good choice. He was also the fifth shooter for his team. Ryan Sheffield was the goalie and fifth shooter for his team. It came down to the final try for both. Ryan missed and Billy scored. I will never forget the sight of my son running, jumping, and cavorting around the field like he had just led the American team to capture the World Cup—whatever that is.

One other sweet and humorous thing about this event involved the trophies. The league leadership had already purchased trophies for every player with the specifics engraved on the plates. There was a thirty minute delay while the team designation plates were swapped between the fourth and fifth place trophies. This trophy is the only one Billy has carried into his manhood. It was a sweet victory for us all. He felt like a winner because he was. I felt like a winner because I had made the best choice of where to be.

I had taken a part-time job driving a contract U. S. Mail truck between Springfield and Joplin on my Mondays off. The contractor lived in Springfield but kept an 80's something Dodge pickup in Joplin. I would drive it to Springfield after church on Sunday nights then get up at 04:00 and drive the bob-tailed truck to the post office for loading. On a strict schedule, I would leave for Joplin, drive 53 M.P.H. and back into the loading dock of the main post office at 06:00. The contract also required two shuttle runs between the main and satellite post offices in the morning and one in the afternoon before the return trip to Springfield. This was a lot of work for 50 bucks but we needed the money and it was the only opportunity God made available for the extra income we needed.

The Would-be Woodsman's annual goal is to find some time to bow hunt in the last week of October. The mail contractor wanted to take off the last week of October and asked me about covering for him. I had one week of vacation coming and took it to drive the mail Monday through Saturday of my favorite week of the year. I think I saw deer along I-44 every morning and evening and I longed to be in the woods but I felt good about my sacrifice. The 300 dollars was very helpful.

I don't want you to think I had not been preparing for the deer season. Archery practice and a couple of scouting forays had been accomplished. I had asked Brad Harris about hunting on the Lohman lease outside Neosho but he, regretfully, had to deny my request. His company was under new ownership. He told me a strip of public land between the road and their lease boundary was open. The local hunters thought it was part of the Lohman leased land and no one was hunting it. I made one pre-season trip there and hung a portable stand in a sprawling oak and walked away. It was not much more than a hundred yards from where I had taken the doe and the fork in previous years.

The mail contractor gave me the Monday after my vacation off. I finally had peace about hunting and sunrise of the Monday before gun season found me in my stand near Neosho. Even though it was my official day off, I needed to do some work at church so I left the stand at 09:00 and scouted around before heading to the vehicle. Three fresh scrapes along the overgrown field edge and timberline got me really excited. They were within view of my stand but out of archery range. I was pleased with the promising situation.

I worked until about one o'clock then headed back south. The 20 mile drive gave me time to consider a different approach to my stand location. I sneaked through the narrow strip of hardwood timber to a spot even with the scrapes then laid a scent trail, dragging a cloth tied to a string and soaked with doe-in-heat urine. It did not smell good to me but I thought it might to the buck, who was obviously in the area. My hope was if he was working through the woodlot he would hit the scent trail and follow it to within bow range. I poured more scent solution in all three scrapes as I passed them and was startled to see a doe rise from her midday bed at the base of my oak tree. She disappeared into the brush—a very good sign.

I spent the next few hours watching, listening, and daydreaming from my stand. A sound which could only have been a buck thrashing a bush with his antlers awakened me from a shallow nap. No deer was visible but he was obviously there, due south of me. I was a little concerned he might detect my scent but I had taken precautions to enter the area clean. A short call from my grunt tube did not elicit an audible response but soon I saw the buck working toward his scrapes.

He took his time and worked all three scrapes with fancy foot work and head rubbing on overhanging limbs. His excruciatingly slow pace allowed my heart rate to settle down, a little. He began to grunt every few steps as he started my way. He walked right up to my tree, obviously looking for the hot doe, and started to circle the tree to my left. That was bad.

I shoot left handed and would have to turn my body at least 90 degrees and there was no good opening for a shot. Unexplainably he stopped, reversed his route, and began to work around to my right. He passed a small cedar tree which I used to conceal the movement of my draw and when he cleared the cedar I let my arrow loose. The range was point blank and my arrow struck high on his right side and angled down. He bolted back the way he had arrived, unaware he was taking my tracking string with him.

As he disappeared from my sight I collapsed against the tree, shaking like I had the flu. I thanked God for the event. I replayed the shot in my mind and recalled the arrow was visible as he vanished into the brush.

That probably meant there would be no exit wound and a tough trail. The string tracker had stopped paying out shortly after I lost sight of the buck, who was wearing a nice rack with ten points visible. Had the string shredded or had the buck gone down? I left the tree and went back to my van.

Brad Harris was guiding for a hunting party nearby so I drove around the corner to his vehicle and waited for them to come out of the woods. He introduced me to his friends and I told him my situation. We agreed on a plan which involved meeting back at my normal parking place after supper. It seemed like forever but I knew Brad was right to let the deer have some time. I called Kathy and told her the reason for my delay.

We met as planned and started working the trail. It was very dark. The string track lasted about 50 yards but there was no buck attached. Not far beyond the end of the string we found the back end of the arrow shaft and a pool of blood where the buck had rolled over and snapped it off. As everyone leaned in to see the shaft and sign we heard the buck get up and go crashing through the brush. He was for sure headed toward the Lohman lease because it was the only option.

Brad said he would normally push the buck a little but he did not want to create a disturbance where they were planning to video a hunt in the morning. He suggested we wait until after the morning hunt and take up the trail again. The weather forecast was for cold and clear. I was agreeable with the plan but it made for a long night.

My boss and pastor granted my request for some time to recover the buck on Tuesday morning. I picked up dozen doughnuts along the way and left them on the hood of Brad's Scout II with a note explaining I could be found working the trail.

It was hard, slow work on my hands and knees. I was stumped at an apparently impenetrable wall of vines and brush. Brad and his hunting video team found me around 9:30. We took up the trail together. The star of Brad's video, a well-known hunting personality, began to circle the obstacle and I crawled in on my belly and immediately found the lost blood trail. This was where the deer had crashed through the previous night. The wall of vines had closed shut like a door behind him.

As I was solving the mystery of the disappearing trail someone called out from the other side of the thicket, "Here's your buck."

To say I was relieved and excited would be a massive understatement. The eleven pointer had lived through the night—evidenced by his body temperature and flexibility. It was a good thing we did not push him the night before. Brad scored the buck at 123 inches, just short of the Pope and Young record book, but he is a trophy for me and my best archery buck to date.

Spending the money or time to mount the buck was out of the question but his antlers on the wall always remind me of priorities chosen and lessons learned. But my late-starting deer season was not over by a long shot.

There were not many opportunities for me to preach at Calvary and never on a Sunday morning. Phillip was rarely gone and there were better, more experienced preachers on staff and in the church. Phillip and I talked often about my call to preach and he was good to allow me to supply preach at other Baptist churches in our area. He felt it was a good way for our large church to encourage and support smaller churches. I agreed and was glad for any opportunity to preach. One such opportunity introduced me to a family who lived deep in

MacDonald County. They liked me and invited me to hunt deer on their Crow Valley farm.

Before dawn of the Saturday after taking the 11 point buck I was up in a tree with Max's Remington 308 on the wooded western slope of Crow Valley. Shortly after sunrise a group of six unantlered deer passed my location and I let them go. They crossed the narrow valley and disappeared up the eastern slope. Soon after, I took a close range shot at a six point buck but appeared to miss. This hunt was my first attempt at hunting with a scope on the rifle. I climbed down and looked in vain for some sign I had even hit the buck. While on the ground a small war broke out to the east where the does had journeyed. I sat down on a large stone at the edge of the woods watched the eastward slope.

I heard them coming long before I saw them. Four does had survived the skirmish with other hunters and were coming back my way. They stopped at a barbed wire fence about a third of the way up from the valley floor. The sun was illuminating their foggy breath. I had a doe permit for the area so I took aim at the largest doe and fired. She dropped immediately. I paced 150 steps to her location and thanked the Lord for success. It was the first doe I had ever taken with a rifle.

I headed for Springfield after Sunday evening services—back to the mail run with a twist. I stayed in Springfield after the Joplin run and accompanied my brother-in-law, Mark Burden, on Tuesday. He was hoping to take a few days off sometime and wanted me to learn his mail route. The route was very complicated and involved ten or more stops over several counties north of Springfield. The sweet part of this deal was my sister would meet us in Stockton after the morning run and we would all go deer hunting on a farm in Hickory County. Mark and Theresa needed some meat for their freezer.

Mark and I took up hopeful positions to watch for deer. I think we both fell asleep. I know I did. We met back at the truck for leftover turkey sandwiches around 10:00 and planned a mini-drive to hopefully stir up some deer activity. We split up and started working north on opposite sides of a wet-weather branch. My side of the creek was thickly wooded with young hardwood growth and I lost sight of Mark and Theresa immediately. After traveling a couple hundred yards I heard a close shot to my left. It had to be Mark. He had spent some time in his life as a Marine marksmanship instructor so I was surprised by two more quick shots and a frustrated yell. He had sold all of his firearms and was hunting with a borrowed 30-30.

His yell was a warning to me and I saw a forked horn buck working his way through the woods a hundred yards to my front. My remaining tag was only good for a buck and he qualified. I took a kneeling position to steady my aim and looked for an opportunity to shoot. He was quartering away from me and would soon be out of sight. He stopped but the only possible shot was at his right hindquarter. I had never intentionally taken a shot at a deer which might not ensure a quick, clean kill. This shot was for meat and for my sister so I took it. The deer went down and did not rise. Fortunately I had hit a major artery and he did not require a second shot.

I had already told Mark and Theresa any deer I harvested would be theirs. He offered to have Sis tag the deer so I could go on hunting. I told him about my 1978 promise to God. My very successful season was over. I had tagged three deer in nine days.

It had been an amazing year for me and my family. I had learned a lot about myself, my faith, my wife, my children, and my church. The more centered and balanced Would-be Woodsman had experienced his greatest success, not just in deer hunting. One more important event needs to be mentioned here. On August 2, Iraqi military forces invaded and quickly conquered the small country of Kuwait. America would lead the response of the world to war with Iraq. I talked with Kathy then called my reserve command and volunteered to go. This war would take our lives in a new direction.

Chapter 20

1991: End of an Era

My offer to volunteer for military activation elicited no response. Several friends from church were alerted and eventually activated with their units. I was not in a reserve unit. I was an Individual Mobilization Augmentee attached to an active duty base for training and support. The war plan called for using us to backfill into stateside base vacancies. Several of my active duty friends from Whiteman AFB had already gone forward. My first experience of the war was working the base mobilization line while on reserve duty and helping the Air Force troops say good bye to their loved ones. It was hard. At home we watched the nightly news—like everyone.

I need to step back a little to put something into perspective here. One Wednesday near the end of summer Kathy and I received a bit of a shock. We were always busy on Wednesday nights with various children's programs and logistical details. We kind of bumped into each other in the fountain foyer outside the main auditorium. We were talking about the kids (making sure we did not leave one of them at the church overnight) or something when the doors opened as adults left the evening prayer service. We were overwhelmed with handshakes and hugs as people told us how they were going to miss us. We looked at each other in puzzled surprise.

The Senior Associate Pastor, Charlie Davidson, informed us what was going on. Phillip had announced I wanted to be pastor of a church and would be leaving to do that as soon as God opened a door. Charlie assured us the pastor had told the church we would stay until that time. The moment had a surreal emotional flashback feeling for us. It reminded us of our experience at Tatum Chapel years before.

One of the deacons and his wife, who were never shy about opposing the pastor (or me by association) stepped close and said to me, "Wayne, don't let your pride make you leave here before you have somewhere to go. You have a family to provide for. Phillip said you could stay as long as you needed to. We'll hold him to it."

It was true Phillip and I had talked much about my future ministry as a pastor but Kathy and I did not see this coming and were shocked at the timing of the announcement. I knew immediately that God was giving me the spiritual maturity test again. It did hurt but I was determined to receive it as from God and not fight or defend myself.

Phillip had been working with a semi-retired church growth consultant out of Texas. He was quickly hired and I began to work for my replacement. I continued to perform faithfully and diligently on any and all projects assigned to me. No opportunity to preach was turned down and I sent my resume all over the place. My new boss, also named Wayne, even worked his contacts as far away as Spokane, Washington, trying to find me a new place to serve. Hopefully these updates from 1990 will help me tell the story of 1991.

Southern Baptist churches traditionally hold special January Bible Studies. I was invited to be a guest teacher for one of these meetings at a nearby rural Baptist church. The name of the church has slipped from my memory but the news someone brought into the building as we closed one evening was big. We were bombing Bagdad!

I hurried home to watch the news. It was a fascinating and exciting time for me but not for my children, especially Billy. The girls said he was crying in his room so I went to see him. His response to my tender query was, "I don't want you to go to Sobby Arabia." I smiled and hugged him, explaining I would most likely be sent somewhere else but even if they did send me to a war area, it would be all right. God would get us through.

The air war continued and I was disappointed my call did not come. Life went on. Wayne's contacts in Spokane began to look hopeful. One possibility was a Baptist church we were familiar with from our military days there. They owned a piece of property in a largely un-churched section of that fine city. They wanted to sponsor a mission church there and I was really interested in non-traditional church planting work. The pastor in Spokane and Wayne began working on a plan to raise financial support. In the meantime, I just kept on plugging away, driving the mail on Mondays and doing whatever was placed in front of me. I did a lot of work on a project to remodel an older but more accessible area of the church and relocate the ministry and administrative staff offices there.

A man in the church had graciously given my family a week of his time share and we had chosen to take a ski trip to northern Idaho during the kids' spring break. It would give us the opportunity to show them Spokane and spend some time with the people there. I was not sure how we were going to pay for the trip but we prayerfully and faithfully planned toward that goal.

One day near the end of the remodeling and relocation project I was paged to take a call. I was on the floor assembling office furniture so someone brought me a phone. It was an official call from the Air Reserve Personnel Center. I was being involuntarily called to active duty in support of Operations Desert Shield and Desert Storm. My orders were in the mail. I was to report to Little Rock AFB on February 14, 1991—just one week away. My immediate emotion was relief, which is a form of gladness.

Things happened fast. I informed Phillip and began to wrap things up in preparation to leave. He asked me to preach the Sunday night before I departed. The church planned a reception after the service.

I was nervous about preaching for some reason and was in my basement office praying diligently when one of the ushers banged on my door. The pastor needed to see me right away in his new office—at the other end of the huge building. I complied immediately and Phillip met me at his office door. He said, "Steve needs to talk to you about something." He looked serious. My mind rushed to remember anything I might have done to offend Steve or his family. I really liked them and they had been great help and deeply moved by the Lord during the Life Action revival.

Phillip led me into his office and Steve was sitting behind the desk. He looked straight at me and said, "I have a problem with you," as he pulled a gun case from beneath the desk. I must have looked so confused he took pity on me and did not press the hoax any further. He smiled and I was glad to see Phillip was actually laughing quietly. Steve said, "Wayne, I appreciate how you have served God here at Calvary. I was going to have this gun cut down to fit me but now I know why I never did. My wife and I want you to have it as a gift."

As he unzipped the case and pulled out a beautiful Remington 700 rifle he continued, "I'm sorry that it is defective, (he paused to enjoy my puzzled look) the bolt is on the wrong side." I immediately remembered a conversation with him from the previous year. My statement that I did not ever expect to ever afford a left-handed rifle reverberated in my mind and I'm sure I was grinning like a child at the best Christmas ever.

He pointed out features like the range-finding scope, leather case, and seventy rounds of .270 ammunition. He put his arm on mine and said, "If you ever need to sell it, it should bring you quite a bit of money." No one had ever given me such a gift and to receive it with no strings attached blew my mind and ruptured my heart. I was speechless. In my spirit I prayed I would never have to sell the gun—such a special gift.

My departure date came quickly. We had breakfast at McDonalds in Webb City as I prepared to leave from there in our 1988 Plymouth Voyager van (The Blue Goose II). Kathy would keep the 1973 Ford LTD two-door (The Tank) Kathy's dad had given us for a second vehicle. I really liked the car but was not sure it would get me to Little Rock and back. Kathy was still working for the car dealership, which had morphed into to a used-car-buy-here/pay-here store. They would take care of her if she needed a vehicle.

It was Valentine's Day so I gave gifts with hugs and kisses then left with a lump in my throat, again. I was sad to leave Kathy and the kids but I was excited to be getting off the bench and into the game. It was also a great relief to be out from under the strained situation at the church. Kathy and I knew this adventure would bring about significant changes for us but we didn't know what.

My experiences in Arkansas had been very limited and I had never given the small state to our south much thought. The five hour drive was enjoyable and I liked what I saw.

When I arrived at Little Rock Air Force Base I discovered three active duty chaplains had been deployed. One chaplain plus a capable NCO Chaplain Support person were with the flying wing of C-130's in Abu Dhabi and two chaplains were at hospitals in Europe. I felt like I was needed and wanted at Little Rock AFB. Another reserve 1Lt. Chaplain from Dover, Delaware arrived the same day. Chris was an energetic Catholic Priest. We both worked hard and enjoyed the challenges.

Not long after our arrival the ground war kicked off in Iraq and was a much greater success than anyone dreamed. It became clear I would not remain on active duty for the one year my orders indicated. I had mixed emotions because the quick victory meant I would be returning home with major unanswered questions about our future.

Speaking of emotions, Kathy and the children made a couple of weekend trips to Little Rock to see me and the area. It was great! She was driving a different vehicle. The first week I was gone she was in a wreck and totaled The Tank. Granted, it didn't take much damage in 1991 to total a 1973 Ford. Max found Kathy a low mileage car which had been traded in Springfield. It was a 1978 Mercury Marquis. Kathy loved this boat-of-a car. The eight track player still worked.

The leader of Chaplain Ministry for the Arkansas Baptist State Convention came to the air base and sought me out. Carter Tucker took me under his wing. When he came to understand the problem I was facing with my ministry setting in Missouri he introduced me to Marvin Peters. Marvin was the Director of Missions for the North Pulaski Baptist Association. He requested I provide him with a current resume. I did and tried not to think too much about it until I was contacted by the Chairman of the Amboy Baptist Church Pastor Search Committee.

The Base Chapel staff was gracious and helpful in getting the committee onto the base to hear me preach one Sunday. We met for a couple of hours after the service. I really liked and enjoyed them but I had a feeling my theological views on race relations would be problematic. Amboy was the only Central Arkansas church who showed any interest. It was time to wrap things up and go home to whatever was there.

I had communicated to my church back in Missouri indicating my return late in April but received no clear response. Unsure of where I stood legally, I made an appointment with an Air Force lawyer. He listened to my story then told me I should be prepared to take legal action against the church when I was discharged. The law was very clear about the employment rights of reservists returning from active duty. I thanked him for his advice but explained I could not follow it. He did not understand even when I explained my belief that citizens of the Kingdom of God should not relate to one another through the courts.

Returning home was bittersweet. There's no place like being home with family but I've never done jobless well. My visit with Phillip and Wayne had not been fruitful. While I was disappointed, I was not surprised. I knew it was time to move on, to something; I just didn't know what.

There was an upside. I was not totally jobless. I picked up the Monday mail run again and was also able to give my brother-in-law a week off as well.

We knew some big change was coming so I worked on our house to get it ready to sell. I rebuilt and improved the rear deck and used the left-over lumber to build the kids a slightly elevated tree house in the woods behind our place.

I was determined to remain faithful to my belief God would take care of us. My plan and desire was to keep a low profile and submissive position regarding the church and my lack of employment. We were still members at Calvary. Kathy and the kids went on—business as usual. God provided me opportunities to preach on most Sundays at other churches. I did not want to be put in a situation where I might say something inappropriate again so I didn't spend much time around church.

One day while working on the house a deacon's wife called me. She and her husband had spoken encouragingly to us on that Wednesday night months before. She straightforwardly asked why I was not working at the church. I told her I did not have a job there. She was angry and asked me some questions I tried to graciously deflect. I did tell her I believed God wanted me to keep a posture of non-self-defense. She encouraged me but indicated she was under no such instruction and had already made inquiries of our congressmen.

Later in the week I received a call from Phillip. He explained that he believed I had resigned when I left for my war assignment. As I have said before, we did not always communicate well. A few days later I received a check for two weeks' salary. It was greatly appreciated.

The ministry possibility in Spokane continued to move forward. I was also surprised to receive more interest from the North Little Rock church. They invited us to come back to Arkansas and engage in a mini-revival meeting. This would give us a weekend to get acquainted.

We made the trip and had a great time. We talked about the possibility of moving there with mixed emotions. Amy, Beth, and Billy were concerned about leaving their friends. Kathy and I were concerned about taking on a struggling church in a neighborhood in transition. There was nothing to do but pray.

Amboy Baptist Church voted to issue me a call to be their pastor. At the same time the situation in Spokane required a decision. It was a tough choice. Should we move our family to Arkansas to be the pastor of a small, declining church with racism issues or move them a couple of thousand miles to a very uncertain situation?

I had learned the church in Spokane had attempted several church starts in the exact place before. The more I talked with the pastor of the mother church the more I realized he would insist on a traditional approach to starting a Southern Baptist church. That was not what I wanted. Kathy and I remembered the conflict between the southern Southern Baptists and the western Southern Baptists at First Baptist Church of Medical Lake. I did not feel right about moving there without the freedom to pursue non-traditional ministry.

After much prayer we accepted the call to Amboy Baptist Church in North Little Rock. The compensation package did not add up to what we thought our needs would be but we believe God is our source and if He was calling us to North Little Rock, He would make a way.

Kathy and the kids had some things to finish up in Joplin but I moved to Arkansas and started at the church on June, 1. Some friends from the air base chapel program invited me to stay at their home in Little Rock. I enjoyed staying with them for the first month then moved in with Tom Warren's family. They lived only a few blocks from the church. His mother, Billie, had been on the Pulpit Search Committee. I quickly fell in love with this family and felt honored to be included with them. Tom was a full-time Army National Guardsman at nearby Camp Robinson.

It was a busy summer for all of us. I was trying to learn to be a good pastor and the honeymoon period was sweet, if short lived. It was a great challenge and adventure for me. While I was busy plowing the new church field Kathy had listed the house in Carl Junction and was trying hard to sell it and get ready to move. I was looking just as hard for a house to rent or purchase so I could move them to Arkansas later in the summer. Neither of us seemed to be having much success on the housing project.

By the middle of July Kathy and I agreed we would move the first week of August no matter what. I was so hungry to have them with me that we would have moved into empty classrooms at church, if nothing else became available. In those weeks I found myself meditating on a verse in Romans, "He staggered not at the promise of God through unbelief, but was strong in faith, giving glory to God, being fully persuaded that what He had promised, He was able also to perform." (Romans 4:20-21) This was referring to Abraham but I claimed it for myself. God had promised if His children seek His kingdom as their prime objective, He will provide everything they need. (Matthew 6:33)

He did. Just days before the move, a church member told me of an open rental house owned by her neighbor's daughter. It seemed perfect to me but I admit to being a little nervous about signing a rental agreement on a house my wife would not see until she was moving in. Talk about faith.

Some Amboy church members helped us with the move. Charles and Lynn Holley made the trip to Missouri with Joe Straw and me. They were a lot of help and a lot of fun. Our train of U-Haul truck, vans, and cars made quite a caravan rolling our way through the Ozarks of southern Missouri and northwest Arkansas.

We had stopped by Calvary Baptist Church for final goodbyes on our way south. We had lots of good memories there and I was satisfied that I had finally passed the test of who to cry to when I felt a Christian brother had offended my easily hurt feelings and sensibilities. It may have been a B- but it was a passing score and I was a pastor now.

As we meandered down Interstate 40 through the Arkansas River Valley we noticed a giant Razorback emblem high on a northern bluff. I had learned in my few months in Arkansas everything seemed to be all about the HOGS. I had a sense, even though we were moving away from our beloved Missouri, we were going home, together—closing one era and opening another. Woo Pig Sooie!

After Thought

(If you have never spent most of a day alone in a deer stand the musings of this article may seem weird to you. If you have never followed the tracks and leavings of an animal in the woods while on your hands and knees you may think this is all foolishness. It is all right. Just don't miss the truth this trace leads to.)

Blood Trail

While slipping slowly and quietly through the forest the woodsman discovers a clearing—a place where a violent scene happened in the past. In the middle of the clearing is a darkly stained post with about six feet of timber rising out of the ground. The woodsman sees two lengths of rope looped through holes high on the post. They are also darkly stained and the woodsman remembers where she has seen that color before—it's dried blood.

Something on the ground to his right catches the corner of the woodsman's eye; it is a length of braided leather—unraveled toward the end. Somehow attached to the ends of these strips of leather are small pieces of bone, stone, and metal. This implement has taken on the same dark, almost-black patina as the post and rope. It is surely an implement of pain and torture.

A pile of debris near the edge of the clearing claims her attention; a strange collection of refuse. Most noticeable among the trash is a large piece of purple cloth. Picking it up by the corner reveals dark stains, no doubt blood. Another interesting piece is what first seems to be a ten-inch vine wreath. Closer examination shows the vines have long, spiky thorns. The spikes of one side of the wreath seem to have been dipped in the same liquid evidenced throughout the scene. The purpose of the post and whip are clear—not so this pile of stuff. One thing is for certain: someone suffered and someone bled here.

A wide, dusty trail leads uphill from the clearing. The woodsman slowly follows to one side, careful not to destroy any evidence. Two or three sets of heavy sandaled footprints line each side of the trail. The size and depth of the tracks indicate they were made by big men. In the middle of the road is one set of barefoot, man-sized prints.

The uneven length of stride and scuff marks on the back trail side of each print indicates this barefoot man is struggling. The woodsman follows the trail up the hill. About ten yards further along the barefoot stride lengthens for a several steps to be followed by several more getting shorter with each stride until the right and left footprints are side by side. Continuing, the woodsman sees this pattern is repeated about every ten steps.

The woodsman looks forward, up the trail, and wonders if the man is carrying a burden, losing his balance as it drives him forward. The woodsman begins to pick up the pace on the easy-to-read track but stops suddenly at a change in the pattern. There is a short drag mark and the footprints are splayed and distorted. About fifteen inches ahead of the footprints are two near perfectly round depressions, maybe 5 inches in diameter. A foot and a half ahead of these circles is a clear left handprint. There is a large square stamped in the dust about a foot to the right of the handprint. The downhill corners of the indentation are deeper.

One other piece of evidence marks this disturbance in the track. To the right of the handprint is a small dark spot on a stone in the roadway. It is black. It is blood. Perhaps this is the trail of the man who was beaten in the clearing.

The track continues and the man goes to his knees more and more often. At some point though, the pattern totally changes. The footprints are often obliterated by a set of large sandaled ones. The bare prints are still there but different, sometimes lightly touching down and sometimes with toes dragging. Two of the outer sets of heavy sandal prints have moved in closer, one set on each side. It appears the injured man is being assisted by his escorts and someone else is carrying the burden—whatever it is. This pattern of sign continues without much variation to the top of the hill.

Here, some questions are answered, some facts become clear. The heavy burden was a roughhewn timber, perhaps seven feet long. It lay on the ground next to a somewhat longer timber. Two other sets of lumber are placed fifteen feet to each side of the pieces the tracks led to. The woodsman notices the timbers are notched to fit together. She sees with her mind's eye these pieces—fitted together—could form a cross. He almost stumbles into a foot wide hole in the ground about three feet deep near the base of the long piece. There are similar holes near the other sets as well, evidently where these crosses were planted and raised from the ground.

She can't help but notice the darks stains—surely blood—around holes in the wood near the ends of each cross piece. There are similar nail holes and stains on the long piece about five feet below the notch. The woodsman has never witnessed one but has heard about them—this must be a scene of execution by crucifixion.

One thing differentiated the center cross from the others; the ground near the hole at the base of the cross was black, stained with blood—lots of blood. Several things are now certain. The man the woodsman followed up the hill suffered here, bled here, and died here.

The woodsman has followed many blood trails before but this one is different—it has shaken him to his core. She wanders around the hilltop for a while before she finds herself following a path down and around its back slope. He eventually finds himself in the middle of an ancient cemetery. Large stones cover the openings of mausoleum-like caves.

One catches her attention and she moves closer. There is a stone but it is rolled back from the opening. He peers in. It is empty. She first thinks it has never been used but her keen woodsman eye notices a lump of cracked and dried clay stuck to the right side of the opening. Curious again, he examines the stone and finds a matching piece of dried clay inverted on the opposite side. Has this grave been used?

Puzzled and excited she looks in again. It is not as empty as he first thought. Over to the left side is a pile of loosely woven cloth. He touches it and finds it stiffened with a salve like substance evidencing a strong but sweet, lingering odor. She notices a smaller, similarly treated piece of cloth on a stone shelf hewn in the side of the room. He is amazed at how neatly it is folded.

Stepping back into the full sunlight the woodsman wonders, "What happened here? What does it all mean?" The woodsman awakens from the trance-like ponderings to find himself seated in a climbing treestand 25 feet above the forest floor. I know you are wondering, "Is the woodsman a man or a woman?" The answer is, "Yes." Woodsmen come in both models.

The woodsman has a unique skill-set including situational awareness, keen observation, and rugged determination. Woods-men and woods-women know where they are and where they want to end up. They recognize and interpret the signs. They stick to the trail and when they temporarily lose it, circle back to where they lost it and try again.

The woodsman's experience and many long hours in the woods convinces them Paul was right when he wrote to the believers in Rome. "For since the creation of the world God's invisible qualities—his eternal power and divine nature—have been clearly seen. Being understood from what has been made, so that people are without excuse." (Romans 1:20)

In their heart-of-hearts every woodsman knows the trees, mountains, flowers, and animal life did not just spring forth on their own. Every woodsman is wise enough to know there is a Creator—a God who loved us so much He sent his one and only Son to conquer life then give up His own in exchange for ours before we ever thought one thought about Him.

The woodsman looks back at his own life-track and into her own heart and knows that God's words to us through an ancient inspired letter to the believers in Rome are true, "All have sinned and fall short of the glory of God." (Romans 3:23) "The wages of sin is death but the gift of God is eternal live through Jesus Christ our Lord. (Romans 6:23) "If you confess with your mouth 'Jesus is Lord' and believe in your heart that God has raised Him from the dead, you will be saved." (Romans 10:9) "For whoever calls on the name of the Lord will be saved." (Romans 10:13)

Every woodsman has been lost in the woods a time or two so we can understand the condition our sin puts us in. Just like those times when the woodsman found the signs which reoriented them toward home, there are signs which can reorient you toward eternal life. These signs are a blood trail, intentionally marked with suffering, love, mercy, grace, and forgiveness. All placed clearly so you can find your way home to God.

Printed in the United States
By Bookmasters